KNOWING OUR
FUTURE

"*Every now and then, a great book comes along that subtly triggers the reader into deep reflection of what was and profound inspiration of what will be. Michael Lee weaves together genius in philosophy, technology, and science from the past few centuries, to create a desperately-needed new system of thinking – Futurology. This book sharpens the lens for seeing the future, as if it were already history.*"
Michael Cushman, Sr. Fellow and Board Member of the futurist think tank, the DaVinci Institute, and author of soon-to-be-released, *The Age of Unlearning.*

"*This is a well-articulated and deeply thoughtful book that reveals the philosophy and logic for the development of the theory for a science of the future. The author combines his specialist knowledge of the futures field with an in-depth grasp of the philosophy of science, so that his work outclasses contemporary social science writings on the art of futures studies. By examining the scientific approaches of pioneers in the futures field, encompassing cosmology, energy resources, population dynamics, economics, social and political science, urbanisation and transportation, and technological development, this deserves to become a popular science classic. More importantly it should be on the reading list for university courses in futurology.*"
Robert H. Samet, author of *Long-Range Futures Research: An application of complexity science.*

"*Michael Lee's startling case for futurology is an impressive and well-informed piece. Follow him on a journey from the early future works from Enlightenment times to contemporary foresight as an academic discipline. And be amazed by what former futurists anticipated, correctly as well as wrongly. In the end, you will know and understand the nature and power of the future.*"
Dr. Pero Mićić, founder of FutureManagementGroup (www.FutureManagementGroup.com)

"Knowing our future *sizzles with bold energy. Michael Lee is to be congratulated for having written a book that explains in an easy to follow format, how the future works. It's both straightforward* to understand and substantive, an unusual combination in our increasingly complex world. Anyone interested in knowing how their future may unfold will find this a must read."

Dick Pelletier, US futurist and founder of PositiveFuturist.com (www.positivefuturist.com).

"As Yogi Berra said, predicting is hard, especially the future. But Michael Lee, founder of the Institute of Futurology and the South African chapter of the World Future Society, has lost patience with the idea that the future is unknowable. He's pretty sure that we denizens of the Twenty-First Century are on the cusp of figuring out how to connect a lot of the dots before the dots even show up. That makes him either a brilliantly prescient observer of human capacities or a supremely self-delusional one. Read Knowing our future and decide for yourself. But be forewarned. Lee's optimism is contagious. He's on a mission, one that matters, especially if he's right."

Dudley Lynch, author of *LEAP! How to Think Like a Dolphin and Do the Next Right, Smart Thing Come Hell or High Water.*

"How delightful it is to read a book about the science and art of long-term prediction which has been so well researched and described in such an entertaining and provocative way. The book also offers sound advice on how we should now look forward into the remainder of this century, having learned from the successes and failures of our predecessors in the futures game."

Clem Sunter, South Africa's top futurist and business thinker and author of *The Mind of a Fox: Scenario Planning in Action.* (www.mindofafox.com)

"Knowing our future is a timely reminder that thinking about the future is essential, especially if you believe that without thinking we might not have much of a future left."

Richard Watson, UK futurist, author, scenario planner and top trends blogger (http://toptrends.nowandnext.com)

For Sannettha, Michaela and Melissa, family and friends for life

MICHAEL LEE

KNOWING OUR
FUTURE

THE STARTLING CASE FOR **FUTUROLOGY**

First published in 2012 by
Infinite Ideas Limited
36 St Giles
Oxford
OX1 3LD
United Kingdom
www.infideas.com

A CIP catalogue record for this book is available from the British Library

ISBN 978–1–906821–98–2

Brand and product names are trademarks or registered trademarks of their respective owners.

Cover design and typesetting: Cylinder

Printed in Britain by TJ International Ltd, Padstow, Cornwall

CONTENTS

LIST OF FIGURES

LIST OF TABLES

FOREWORD

When you look at a chessboard you notice it has 8 squares across and 8 squares down, giving a total of 64 squares:

Now imagine covering half of the board with a white cloth and showing it to someone else:

Using pattern recognition, this person would be able to predict what the rest of the covered board looks like. What about a more complex shape like a kaleidoscope pattern?

The same exercise would be more difficult, but still very doable:

Unless, that is, you covered up most of the picture:

At this point, some guess-work will be needed to draw the whole pattern and there is insufficient information to get it exactly right. The design in the centre, for example, is absent from the partial version so someone looking at it will not know how to reconstruct the obscured section of the picture.

Future-watching, as you will discover in the following pages, is a form of pattern recognition (see Figure 15). Drawing on laws of nature and laws of history, and integrating as much information as possible about a given society or system, it is possible to recognise patterns of time which will be completed sometime in the future. We can build up accurate foreknowledge of the world of tomorrow by identifying the causes and conditions shaping today's world, in a living and largely predictable process of transition, into the society of the future. The more current knowledge we have, the more foreknowledge we can preconstruct.

This book provides a theory of how foreknowledge can be logically gained as part of a science of the future called futurology. In its pages, you will come across strange concepts and terms like space-time, 4-D reality, the relativity of time, time dilation, as well as prognostication, preconstruction and foreknowledge. Getting to know these concepts may become an adventure of the mind. I certainly hope so. You will also follow the story of humanity's long search for a science of the future.

What is incontestable is that we do have within our grasp the tools and theoretical principles to support a discipline of futurology. Prognostic thinkers from Marquis de Condorcet to H.G. Wells pointed the way to this science of the future. Today there are sound scientific, philosophical and logical grounds for believing we can systematically explore and know the future. The benefits of doing this are obvious: reducing fear of the unknown, better planning, more sustainable long-term strategies, improved forcasting, fewer socio-economic crises, sounder investment decisions, etc.

The story and theory of futurology are offered here not only to support these goals but to inspire readers to become proactive thinkers, people who embrace the future boldly.

Michael Lee
Cape Town, 2012

ACKNOWLEDGEMENTS

The best feature of our home in Cape Town is a rooftop terrace from which we can look out over mountain ranges of the Western Cape soaring over an undulating, vineyard-studded landscape. The terrace and the stone steps leading up to it were built by the previous owners of the house.

To see into the future you need a mental rooftop as your vantage point. The joy of conducting this study into the theoretical and methodological grounds for foreknowledge is that the steps leading to the rooftop had already been built by intellectual giants and thinkers like Einstein, Bohm and Stephen Hawking in physics, Russell, Whitehead, Keynes and Peirce in philosophy, Jevons, Hubbert and Ayres in the field of industrial energy, Sorokin in sociology, Morris in history, Marquis de Condorcet, H.G. Wells and Robert Samet in long-range social prognostication, and Kondratieff and Schumpeter in economics.

I want to thank David Grant and his team at Infinite Ideas in Oxford for their innovative approach to publishing in today's hyper-competitive world of books. Dawn Sackett provided highly effective copy editing. Thanks, too, to complexity scientist Robert Samet for invaluable mentorship and for believing this work to be an interesting contribution to theory-building in the study of the future. Elisabeth Dostal's Biomatrix systems theory proved inspirational.

It was a lonesome yet deeply inspiring journey producing this study. So sincere thanks are due to my wife and daughters to whom this book is dedicated for lovingly accepting the complex guy in their midst who was too abstracted for far too long during its creation.

I would like to thank all the publishers who granted me licence to reuse excerpts from their publications, as well as authors, including Dr Robert Samet and Dr Elisabeth Dostal, for their personal permission to quote from their important works. I would especially like to thank Profile Books for their permission to use quotes free-of-charge from *Why the West Rules for Now* by Ian Morris. If I have unintentionally left out any publisher from my list of copyright permissions, I would be happy to rectify that omission in subsequent editions of the text.

CHAPTER 1
THE LENS OF TIME

We tend to approach the future tentatively, assuming it is unknowable, beyond the reach of our mental powers. Yet below the surface of daily events flows the endless progress of time in which everything in the universe evolves through an ordered sequence of states towards its final purpose.

Physics, drawing upon Einstein's special relativity, has unveiled much of the mystery of time. It has proved, for example, that time travels in one direction only, towards our future, despite the fact that there's nothing in nature's laws preventing physical processes from happening in reverse order. It has revealed that space and time are united in one four-dimensional world. We can understand time, and, consequently, the future, better than ever before.

The laws of nature have been mapped out in exquisite detail. This enables accurate predictions to be made about its behaviour, including the destiny of the universe itself. Everything that exists has a lifespan characterised by cycles of birth, growth and eventual decline. There is evidence of an infinite array of patterns of life, endlessly repeating themselves in a breathtaking cosmic kaleidoscope.

In addition, there is a deep structure to history, a discernible sense of its laws which underpin social development. The fortunes of societies and civilisations fluctuate while they evolve, following principles and patterns evident throughout history. Recurrent, long-wave economic and business cycles have been identified and analysed. Commodities from gold to oil are discovered, produced and then peak, after which sharp declines in production invariably occur, accompanied by rising prices. Even the cycle of exponential growth of computer power, currently doubling every eighteen months, is predicted to end by around 2020, due to limits imposed by nature.

Viewed through the lens of time, life on all levels, from cosmological to social, behaves with regularity and purpose, allowing us to estimate its future course.

In the last few decades, systems thinking has developed models explaining how systems operate and interact across the whole spectrum of nature and society. This has opened up a rich treasure chest of theoretical insight. Since virtually everything in the universe is made up of systems and sub-systems, from our bodies to the solar system, these advances in understanding how the world works (and how it will continue to work in the future) are far-reaching.

As a result of significant gains in knowledge across many fields of enquiry, humanity now has at its disposal sufficient understanding of time, history, systems, lifecycles and laws of nature to explore the future in a systematic way. Instead of being one of humanity's most neglected assets, the future should become the next frontier of knowledge. A scientific study of the future is possible.

The future can be studied and understood as systematically as the past. Forecasts will perhaps never quite contain the level of detail of historical information but we do not need to know every detail about the future in order to understand or predict it. The future is history-in-the-making just as history is the future-in-the-making. What we need to know about the future are conditions and causal factors shaping events and social evolution according to universal laws and principles within the most probable time spans. Using the right tools and skills, we can paint pictures of the world of the future which are accurate and illuminating. We can construct plausible portraits of the coming times. With increasing visibility, we can see the future.

The main challenge, which has always been the most difficult aspect of looking into the future, lies in effectively integrating knowledge from different disciplines in science and the social sciences in order to lay a comprehensive groundwork for predictions of a complex social future. Yet this is by no means an insurmountable obstacle.

As a futurist, I was taught to believe that the future cannot be known, given that it is non-factual and not-yet-real. Grasping Einstein's revelations about time, and its relationship to space, however, set off a chain reaction in my mind which led to an overthrow of the misconception that the future is unknowable. The purpose of this book is to explain why, how and to what degree we can know the future. It provides a theory showing how to build foreknowledge in order to organise for the future.

A science of the future would enable governments to formulate more sustainable, forward-looking policies. It would improve long-term strategic planning for organisations. Understanding the future would better prepare individuals, organisations and societies to face relentless forces of change. It would reverse stagnation in social, political and economic development arising from uncertainty of the future. It would make for better investment decisions and for greater stability in business. It would make systems everywhere more efficient and sustainable, paving the way for improved future performance. The days of stumbling blindly from one socio-economic crisis to another would gradually fade into the mists of time. Humanity would no longer be defenceless in the face of destiny.

Neuropsychological evidence has revealed that the human brain has a unique capacity, located in one core neural network, to engage in mental time travel into the past and future: 'Ulric Neisser speaks of the three phases of the "perceptual cycle", each of which corresponds to a faculty of the mind: memory of the immediate past, perception of the immediate present, and imagination or foresight of the immediate future. These three faculties are not viewed as independent, but as interacting parts of a single process.'[1]

It is thought that foresight could be our most effective evolutionary tool for long-term survival and mastery of our environment. It is not just that foresight is a fundamental human skill. But we have amassed sufficient understanding of how the world works to produce real foreknowledge which anticipates future social conditions.

It is as if our brains have been preparing for centuries to house and manipulate this knowledge of the future. The study of memory in psychology looks at both retrospective and prospective memory, 'the ability to formulate plans and intentions, to retain them, and to execute them'.[2] Significantly, these two functions are intertwined in the human mind: 'In recent years, evidence has accumulated that the episodic memory system is also involved in mental travel into the future....The primary role of episodic memory, then, may be to provide information from the past for simulation of the future....Foresight...is arguably our most formidable weapon.'[3]

To support compelling insights from physics and neuropsychology about the nature of time and of mental time travel, we need an epistemology of the future to explain the methodology by which valid knowledge of the future may be obtained.

A proper theory of futurology, based on scientific and logical principles, could lead to the creation of next generation knowledge-based systems and societies. It would make possible the permanent shift from a reactive to a proactive frame of mind. It could help humans to feel more in control of their destinies, underpinning a new boldness. An epistemology of the future, in short, may bring about breakthroughs for knowledge and for human consciousness.

In pre-modern times, humans tried to understand the apparent mystery of the future through prophecy, oracles, premonitions and divination. There has always been a need to feel connected, however vaguely, to the future, perhaps to reduce fear of the unknown.

In this generation, humanity may finally be in a position to replace apprehension about the future with a confidence based on better understanding of how it works. Future shock should dissipate in the light of foreknowledge, defined as awareness of something before it happens or exists. Memories of the future will then take shape in our minds.

It was the pioneers of prognostic thinking in Europe, from the time of the French Revolution through the nineteenth century, writing with astounding prescience, who laid the foundations for the emergence of a science of the future. These writers, Marquis de Condorcet, Thomas Malthus and W. Stanley Jevons, in particular, correctly made long-range predictions of such future phenomena as the rise of women's rights, the end of slavery, the emergence of globalisation, the threat of famines which have blighted parts of the world in modern times, as well as the eventual loss of Britain's global economic supremacy as a result of diminishing domestic coal supplies. They also made some erroneous predictions based on faulty assumptions.

Even though theories of the social future developed by these early modern prognostic thinkers were incomplete and even immature, they do prove that it *is* possible to produce prognostic knowledge of the society of tomorrow. Their accurate long-term social forecasts were not flukes or wild guesses. On the contrary, they were based on sound theoretical principles about what shapes the future. There is no reason why such successful social forecasts may not be reproduced at will, if the underlying theory behind the predictions is correct and complete.

Futurists today can build on these promising beginnings. The trail-blazing achievements in foresight discussed in the next two chapters demonstrate that foreknowledge is within our cognitive reach. We have acquired much more advanced knowledge of the key drivers of future conditions. We have irrefutable evidence that time and space go together in one continuum which will deliver one future for us all. There is nothing stopping us from producing as much foreknowledge as we need.

CHAPTER 2
PIONEERING A SCIENCE OF THE FUTURE

It was during the turmoil of the French Revolution that the idea of a modern approach to the future was born. At the time, the Enlightenment movement put forward a doctrine of social progress fuelled by scientific knowledge and the power of human reason. Progress, a cardinal idea of modern times, presupposes the future, pointing towards a better world brought about by knowledge-based social development.

In this phase of turbulent historic change, Marquis de Condorcet accurately predicted the rise of equal rights for women just under a century before it came to pass. This was an amazing feat of foresight. Although he cannot be described as a futurist, Condorcet (1743–1794), was certainly a prognostic thinker. He anticipated the increase of political equality in a new era in which scientific knowledge, allied to liberty, was destined to play a decisive role in society.

A French mathematician, philosopher and political scientist, Condorcet concluded his study of the history of humanity's intellectual and moral development with a chapter on the future progress of mankind as he foresaw it.

In this penetrating look into the far future, he wrote, with unconcealed passion: 'Among those causes of human improvement that are of the most importance to the general welfare, must be included, the total annihilation of the prejudices which have established between the sexes an inequality of rights, fatal even to the party which it favours....And here we may observe, how much the abolition of the usages authorised by this prejudice, and of the laws it has dictated, would tend to augment the happiness of families....' [4]

British suffragette Mary Wollstonecraft published *A Vindication of the Rights of Women* in 1792, but the first country to grant women suffrage in national elections was New Zealand in 1893, just under a century after the posthumous publication of Condorcet's treatise on progress.

In addition to predicting the rise of women's rights several decades before it happened, Condorcet also foresaw the coming of an extensive economic globalisation process: 'the moment knowledge shall have arrived at a certain pitch in a great number of nations at once, the moment it shall have penetrated the whole mass of a great people, [a] whole language shall have become universal, and the whole commercial intercourse shall embrace the whole extent of the globe'. [5]

Again, these words, perhaps history's first definition of globalisation, are profoundly foresightful. How did Condorcet correctly anticipate both the establishment of the right of women to vote in national elections, almost a century before it happened, and the rise of a highly integrated global economy a century and a half ahead of its time? The answer is: he based these forecasts on a theory of dynamic social change developed through long-range historical analysis. He believed in the evolution of society towards perfection through the acquisition and application of knowledge. [6] True to Enlightenment philosophy, he argued that the tools of progress were science, education and the use of human reason leading to increased emancipation and moral development. [7]

Importantly, Condorcet was convinced that there were laws of social development analogous to natural laws: 'The only foundation of faith in the natural sciences is the principle, that the general laws...which regulate the phenomenon of the universe, are regular and constant; and why should this principle, applicable to the other operations of nature, be less true when applied to the development of the intellectual and moral faculties of man?' [8]

One of these social laws, he argued, was that universal access to knowledge would engender political equality and freedom. He was convinced there would eventually be equality between sexes, races and classes in society. Slavery, oppression of women and the institution of the monarchy were all destined to disappear, since modern civilisations, in his view, would advance at the expense of inequality.

What made his prognostications so revolutionary was that they were grounded, not in divination or intuition, but on a theory of social evolution, derived from evidence found in history. [9] In particular, Condorcet argued that a self-reinforcing, or virtuous, cycle would emerge whereby education becomes more widespread in society, leading to more equal wealth distribution through higher levels of social equality, which, in turn, would continue to widen the spread of knowledge. Liberty and knowledge, in other words, would mutually reinforce one another in the process of social development. He rightly believed that this virtuous cycle would bring about large-scale change to society. Any such self-reinforcing process, whether virtuous or vicious, will cause widespread and rapid change.

While Condorcet correctly identified some real drivers of future social progress, he never developed a comprehensive theory of the future. Focused on socio-political advancement, his forecasts do not encompass factors like technology or the environment. He paid only superficial attention to economic principles. Ultimately, his theory of social change, however powerful, is pre-modern in its neglect of the role of technology and its weak use of economic causal factors of social advancement.

Nevertheless, we are witnessing here the birth-pains of a science of the future. Condorcet's ground-breaking 1795 work is the most influential early study of the future of society based on a theory of laws of social evolution. It inspired many competing theories of social change, the first, and most controversial of which, was the more pessimistic, population-based, approach of Thomas Malthus.

Malthus (1766–1834), a clergyman and economist, wrote *An Essay on the Principle of Population* in 1798 just a few years after Condorcet had died in prison under suspicious circumstances following his arrest as a perceived ideological threat to the revolutionary French government. Malthus argued that population growth in the long-run tended to outrun a country's means of subsistence, especially its food production rate.

If Condorcet erred in his prognostications on the side of idealism, Malthus is seen as a voice of pessimism. Futurists, it may be noted, should embrace neither optimism nor pessimism (see Chapter 14). Both perspectives may lead to 'de-futuring', that is, being passive towards the future. Pessimists and optimists are often blindsided by important drivers of change located beyond their theoretical paradigms.

Malthus' core proposition was that population growth should be kept down to the level of a country's means of subsistence. [10] He did not share Condorcet's view of unlimited linear progress [11] towards perfection. He saw history, rather, as an endless series of economic cycles.

Economists such as Nikolai Kondratieff and Joseph Schumpeter have demonstrated that there are, indeed, long economic waves, lasting approximately sixty years, of boom and bust. The latest evidence for the existence of these long-wave economic cycles is the global credit crisis of 2008–2009, a collapse almost comparable to the Depression years just under eight decades earlier.

Like Condorcet, Malthus based his future projections on laws of nature he believed were applicable to social development. He postulated that the needs for food and sex are the two basic drivers of human existence, constituting 'fixed laws of our nature'. [12] Malthus then put forward his main proposition: 'the power of population is indefinitely greater than the power in the earth to produce subsistence for man. Population, when unchecked, increases in a geometrical ratio. Subsistence increases only in an arithmetical ratio'. [13]

Malthus thought the geometric rate of population growth, with population tending to double every twenty-five years, would always outstrip the capacity of the land to produce food. This was because food production increased at a slower, arithmetical rate. Respected archaeologist Joseph Tainter cites a growing disjunction between food production in a stressed environment and population growth as one cause of the collapse of the Mayan civilisation between AD 790 and 890. [14]

For Malthus, this recurrent social problem of a stressed food production system undermined the whole idea of the perfectibility of human progress as propounded by Condorcet and other Enlightenment thinkers. He predicted that times of famine lay ahead for a large portion of the human race. Malthus reminds us to think about what he called the 'modesty of nature'. This principle of limited resources provides a much-needed reality check for all thinking about the future.

Although there are flaws in his demographic projections, it has proved true that starvation and malnutrition have haunted the modern era amidst all the signs of progress, including the Great Irish Famine of 1846–1851, the Ethiopian famine of 1888–1891, the Soviet famine of 1931–1933, the Great Chinese Famine of 1959–1961, as well as famines in Biafra in the late 1960s, Ethiopia in 1984–5 and North Korea in the 1990s, to mention only a few.

Malthus' negative projections for Britain, however, proved inaccurate. He predicted that within one hundred years from the time of writing, the population would increase from 7 million to 112 million. However, the means of subsistence would support only 35 million people, leaving a population of 77 million 'totally unprovided for'. [15] This doomsday scenario never materialised. Britain's population peaked at around 60 million, and the twentieth-century Green Revolution increased the capacity to produce food on a mass-production scale. At the same time, birth control became prevalant and more sophisticated.

Malthus was one of the first modern thinkers to highlight limits to future economic growth when making long-range forecasts. By so doing, he extended our knowledge of the future. While Condorcet foresaw an impossibly positive future, Malthus saw an improbably bleak one. Somewhere between idealistic projections of this nature and prophecies of doom will lie the most probable future.

These two early studies of long-range social forecasts predicted aspects of the future with considerable success. In the late eighteenth century, though, the modern approach to the future was still in its infancy and fraught with theoretical limitations.

Then there was a giant step forward. In the second half of the nineteenth century a British economist discovered that industrial energy was the real driver of social and economic progress.

CHAPTER 3
UNLOCKING THE FUTURE OF SOCIETY

In his 1865 book *The Coal Question* British economist and logician W. Stanley Jevons forecast the depletion of Britain's coal mines during the ensuing one hundred years. Jevons correctly identified the crucial role of industrial energy in determining a nation's socio-economic future.

It is no surprise that some of the most successful forecasts of the distant future ever made have been in the field of industrial energy. These successes are due primarily to the major role of energy in all economies and in all systems. In addition, non-renewable energy sources, such as the fossil fuels of oil, gas and coal, are finite. That enables analysts to quantify future supply and demand scenarios which can be very accurate.

The Coal Question is one of the best works of factual foresight ever written. The book's sub-title, *An Inquiry Concerning the Progress of the Nation, and the Probable Exhaustion of our Coal Mines*, describes the gist of his argument that future depletion of Britain's industrial energy sources could harm its social progress.

Whereas Condorcet identified education as the major driver of progress, and Malthus focused on the effects of population growth relative to food production, Jevons contended that energy production was the source of industrial and economic progress. [16]

Jevons wrote glowingly of the 'incredible' power contained in coal.[17] He rightly maintained that energy underpinned both nature and economies: 'the universe, from a material point of view, is one great manifestation of a constant aggregate of energy...these views lead us at once to look upon all machines and processes of manufacture as but the more or less efficient modes of transmuting and using energy'.[18] This statement is a milestone in the human search for knowledge of the future. It expresses the view that energy powers both the universe and economies. I concur.

Britain's coal-fuelled economic growth had increased its prosperity *and* social cohesion. Jevons feared that the decline of coal supplies and increased costs of mining would reverse this commercial progress. Unemployment and falling standards of living would ensue.

Jevons described his country's coal resources as the 'mainspring of material modern civilisation…coal is all-powerful….It is the material source of the energy of the country – the universal aid – the factor in everything we do…the sole necessary basis of our material power'. [19] It was, he said, an Age of Coal. Furthermore, he argued that there was no known substitute for 'coal as a source of heat and power'. [20] He foresaw a future 'limit to the increase of our wealth'. [21]

Given that British coal fuelled the nation's wealth creation, and that its supply was finite, a socially threatening energy crunch lay ahead. As coal mines were depleted, so the cost of coal extraction would rise: 'the growing difficulties of management and extraction of coal in a very deep mine must greatly enhance its price. It is by this rise of price that gradual exhaustion will be manifested, and its desperate effects occasioned'. [22] These higher economic costs of coal mining would trigger negative social consequences. Price increases of a key energy resource would reverse material prosperity and lead to commercial decline.

At the heart of his remarkable one hundred year forecast is the assumption of a causal relationship between diminishing supply and increased costs. As coal resources declined and production peaked, prices would escalate. Eventually, mining would become unprofitable and supplies would be exhausted. Jevons calculated the rise in coal prices based on projecting consumption rates and estimated the average depth of coal mines in a hundred year time-frame. He calculated the aggregate of British coalfields to be 79,843 million tons with a total of 83,544,000,000 tons of available coal. [23] He forecast that the total aggregate consumption of the period of 110 years, 1861–1970, would be 102,704,000,000 tons, compared to an estimated 83,000,000,000 tons available to a depth of 4,000 feet. [24] He then worked out total supply relative to total demand. Based on expected future consumption rates he concluded that all the available supply would last a total of 212 years before absolute exhaustion by the year 2075.

His concern, however, was that long before 2075, the British manufacturing industry, lacking competitively priced energy, would have lost its economic supremacy to other nations. He was thinking of America with its coalfields 'thirty-seven times more extensive than ours'. [25] Once the price of British coal exceeded that of American coal, the impact on trade was going to be severe.

As a result of declining supply, rising demand and increased costs of its most important industrial energy source, Britain's economic growth was destined to peak and then decrease. [26] Jevons realised there were absolute limits to the supply of fossil fuel energy sources which erected a ceiling to wealth creation based on these sources. [27]

Jevons noted that Britain's portion of world coal production had fallen from sixty percent to twenty-seven percent in only forty-three years.[28] Just over ninety years after the publication of *The Coal Question*, US geophysicist M. King Hubbert confirmed that the production pattern for world coal production had, as anticipated by Jevons, peaked, leading to sharp declines in the post-peak period. He explained: 'coal has been mined continuously for about 800 years, and by the end of 1955 the cumulative production for all of this time was 95 billion metric tons. It is somewhat surprising, however, to discover that the entire period of coal mining up until 1925 was required to produce the first half, while only the last thirty years has been required for the second half.' [29] Hubbert illustrated the steep decline in production of coal after 1925, confirming the general accuracy of Jevons' main thesis regarding Britain's anticipated 'Peak Coal'.

Surprisingly, Jevons totally underestimated the future role of oil: 'Petroleum has, of late years, become the matter of a most extensive trade…[but] its natural supply is far more limited and uncertain than that of coal….' [30] He had a blind-spot in his vision of the future, being unable to see beyond a coal-powered world. For him there was no life beyond coal as the supreme energy source. He even wrongly predicted that steam-engines would still be used a hundred years hence. [31]

In the study of social prognostications, we will see repeatedly how ideology and preconceptions often block out the examination of alternatives in futuristic visions. Futurology needs to eliminate the filter of ideology altogether in order to become fully scientific.

Unbeknownst to Jevons, the Age of Oil was about to begin. It was destined to eclipse industrial progress brought about during the Age of Coal. Britain would discover huge North Sea oil and gas reserves in the early 1970s which would fuel prosperity for the nation beyond its Peak Coal milestone. This highlights the point that incomplete knowledge can limit the accuracy and effectiveness of long-range forecasts. Predictions need to be based on sound theoretical assumptions *and* sufficiently wide-ranging factual knowledge. Jevons did not know that Britain would become an important oil producer because he was writing decades before North Sea oil reserves were discovered. But he should have foreseen the rise of oil as an energy source and recognised its vast global industrial potential.

Jevons looked far ahead in time to Britain's Peak Coal milestone. He wanted his nation, in the 'fat years' of prosperity, to prepare for declining material standards of living in future 'lean years'. He advised against the expenditure of current material wealth on 'increased luxury and ostentation and corruption'. Instead, he urged investment in 'raising the social and moral condition of the people, and in reducing the burdens of future generations'. [32] He saw connections between a nation's manufacturing and commercial power and its social, intellectual and moral progress. Like Condorcet and Malthus before him, Jevons extended the human capacity for understanding the future. He introduced energy as a driver of economic and social progress.

Energy does, indeed, drive growth and progress. It's fundamental to the health and growth of systems in both nature and society. American economist Robert U. Ayres has identified the role of energy, and its conversion into what he calls useful work and production, as a primary causal factor in economic development: 'I conceptualize the economy as a processor and converter of material resources, first into an intermediate good called "useful work". Useful work then converts nonfuel raw materials into finished materials, material products, and eventually nonmaterial services.' [33] The energy applied in work converts raw materials into material products which, in turn, generate non-material business services. This can be visualised in a diagram.

Figure 1 illustrates that the whole process of economic conversion and production is fuelled by energy. Ayres described the ratio between useful work output and raw energy input from fuels, or other natural sources, as the conversion efficiency.

Ayres considered the key to economic growth to be the cost of power and energy and the associated efficiency ratio of conversion of energy into work and production. Improvements in energy conversion via engines, turbines and so on, he argued, lead to a decrease in the cost of primary products; and a corresponding decrease in prices and increase in demand and scale of production, which leads to further cost reductions. [34] Energy, according to both Jevons and Ayres, makes the economic world go round: 'Energy is concerned in all the actions of nature and technics.' [35]

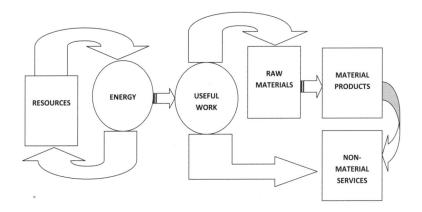

Figure 1. Energy driving the engine of the economy

Source: Author's diagram based on Robert Ayres' concept of the economy as a processor and converter of materials into useful work and production

Technologists repeatedly stress the role of thermodynamic energy in developing social and economic systems: 'It is through expenditure of energy that we convert all raw materials into use forms and operate all the equipment which we use. It is through expenditure of energy that we live....The fundamental physical concept for relating and measuring all forms of physical activity is that of work, or energy expended.' [36] The intense power of fossil fuel energy, and its conversion efficiencies, led to the creation of the technological infrastructure of modern society. [37]

The absolute dependence of economies and societies upon energy is incontestable. In today's world, we face Peak Oil. [38] This is an energy-based challenge unparalleled in the 5,500 year history of civilisation. With global oil production now at its peak, it will be useful to illustrate oil's flow of influences throughout the global economy.

Figure 2 shows the significant dependency of the transport sector on oil. In turn, important economic sectors and processes depend upon transport. Ultimately, productivity, consumption and economic growth all rely heavily on the supply and price of oil.

This chapter has shown that it is a law of progress that economic growth depends upon the efficient exploitation of energy sources. Jevons deserves to be regarded as a major theoretical economist for illustrating this law in *The Coal Question*. He based his forecasts about Britain's future Peak

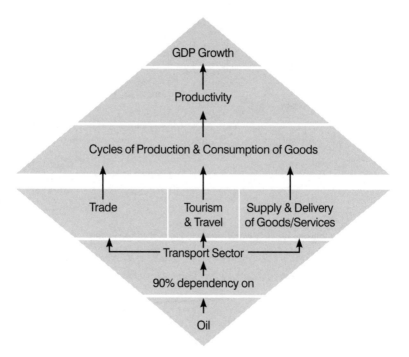

Figure 2. Dependence of economy on oil

Coal, and the social decline he feared it would bring about, upon this law. In short, he unlocked the secret of the social future.

Not even Jevons, however, was free of ideological presuppositions. As previously noted, he could not see beyond the Age of Coal. He failed to foresee the coming Age of Oil. In fact, none of the early prognostic thinkers we have studied so far produced ideology-neutral analyses of the future. Nevertheless, their underlying theories of progress did generate several telling social predictions of the long-range future.

A similar pattern may be seen in the next pioneer of an evolving science of the future, the science fiction writer and social thinker, H.G. Wells. More than anyone else, he invented the modern discipline of studying the social future.

CHAPTER 4
INVENTING THE FUTURE

In his 1901 non-fiction work *Anticipations*, H.G. Wells showed that it was possible for a new discipline of futurology to produce really useful sociological foresight. *Anticipations*, although flawed in that its ideological bias is excessive, certainly extended our theoretical understanding of the social future developed by far-sighted prognostic thinkers like Condorcet, Malthus and Jevons.

H.G. Wells, like Jules Verne before him, thought deeply and imaginatively about the future. He was able to draw on the work of the late-eighteenth and nineteenth-century pioneers of futures thinking. *Anticipations* is his most explicitly futurist book. In it, he developed a systematic long-range study of the future for the whole of the twentieth century. The book's stated aim was to outline 'a rough sketch of the coming time…[an] anticipatory balance-sheet'.[39] Wells set out to construct a 'picture of a human community somewhere towards the year 2000'.[40] *Anticipations* presented a one hundred year vision of society for the century that was just beginning. The point of departure for Wells' vision of the future was that transportation systems constitute the most critical catalyst for broad social development: 'upon transport, upon locomotion, may also hang the most momentous issues of politics and war'. [41]

Wells regarded the steam engine,[42] for example, as the dominant transport technology of the nineteenth century in Britain. He explained that cities and towns had developed around key transport, or transit nodes, creating a 'railway world'. [43] He stated that 'the general distribution of population in a country must always be directly dependent on transport facilities'. [44]

Based on this logic, he predicted that new motorised vehicles, namely trucks carrying goods, motor omnibuses transporting people *en masse* and privately owned motor vehicles, would create new transportation systems. There would be widespread development of roads specifically for motor vehicle use. Horse-driven transport would be banned from these new roads after a legislative campaign. Vast new urban regions would develop further inland along the nodes of this road system.

Wells quantified how the motor transport systems he envisaged would determine population distribution. He used the principle that the maximum journey to work in the city would be two hours. The radius of urban growth based on horse-driven transport systems had been limited to 7–8 miles, whereas the railways could extend this distance to about 30 miles. By the year 2000, Wells believed, this radius would reach 100 miles due to the new motorised transport systems. This would create suburbs for London stretching north to Nottingham and east to Exeter.

These predictions of a pattern of urban growth based around motor transport systems were accurate. Wells correctly envisaged huge urban regions centred in cities and reaching out into a web of suburbs along lines mapped out by road and railway systems. [45] We still live today in the motorised world predicted by Wells in *Anticipations*.

However, Wells incorrectly assumed that this mass diffusion of the British population would solve the problem of congestion in London and in other cities. He underestimated the growth in high-rise buildings on prime urban land, a factor which mitigated against the diffusion he predicted. Suburban diffusion along lines carved out by new road systems for motor vehicles *did* happen but complete decongestion in major cities did *not* happen.

While this pioneer futurist was correct that twentieth-century societies would be heavily motorised, characterised by road systems carrying trucks, buses and cars in the same way that the previous century had been a 'railway world', he did not foresee the sheer scale of modern society's dependence upon motorisation. Nor did he envisage how the oil industry, fuelling motorisation, would become a key aspect of the geo-political landscape of the century ahead.

His theory of transport, the 'available means of transit', [46] as a key driver of social and urban development is generally correct but one-sided. It overlooks the indispensable role of energy sources and supplies in all systems, including transportation. The role of oil in politics has become critical ever since the 1973 OPEC oil embargo crisis. Wells failed to account for the dependence of all industrial systems, including transportation, upon energy. He should have read Jevons.

This theoretical shortcoming illustrates the principle that any incorrect, or one-dimensional, theory of plausible causation for future effects will produce deficient or, at best, partially correct forecasts. To build a theory of social development on the foundation of transportation, while failing to analyse possible impacts of the energy source without which that system cannot operate, was bound to introduce some degree of short-sightedness into Wells' general social forecasts. Forecasts are only as good as the assumptions underpinning them.

Wells also foresaw that new roads for motorised transport would bring about alternative distribution channels for products and services. New communication systems through the telephone service, he argued, would shrink distance just as surely as roads and railways. As a committed socialist and member of the Fabian Society, he projected his faith in state institutions into this space opening up in transport and communications when he predicted that the post office would deliver not only post but products up to a distance of a hundred miles from each of its branches. He believed that customers would phone the post office and order goods to be home delivered. Yet over a century after the publication of *Anticipations*, households still do the bulk of their shopping at retail outlets, although internet shopping is growing. It is fair to say that Wells' forecast that the post office would become a huge national retailer did not come true. The science fiction writer foresaw the potential for mass delivery of products to homes. He just got the delivery channel wrong.

Wells correctly predicted the coming of aeroplanes but failed to recognise the scale by which this technology would revolutionise global transportation. He simply mentioned that once there were aeroplanes they would be applied immediately to war. [47] Yet aeroplanes 'shrank' the world and helped create a more globalised society in ways he did not envisage.

Wells reasoned that a huge new interconnected urban middle class, created by the dominant technology of motorisation, would generate a plurality, or fragmentation, of moralities. There would be greater variety of sexual and family relationships in the new order, in which church authority would wane. Wells correctly forecast that the twentieth century would witness a moral relaxation and greater permissiveness: 'It is foolish…not to anticipate and prepare for a state of things when not only will moral standards be shifting and uncertain…but also when vice and depravity, in every form that is not penal, will be practised in every grade of magnificence and condoned.' [48] He spoke of an 'impending dissolution of a common standard of morals' as there was no 'way or hope of attaining unanimous truth anymore'. [49] Time has proven these words to be prescient.

The widening of the educated class in modern society would, he believed, hasten the arrival of this pluralistic society. He identified the rise in the level of general intelligence within a nation as a precondition for social progress, seeing education as one of the shaping forces of society.

This belief led Wells to prematurely forecast the demise of Russia due to its high levels of illiteracy. Its 'illiterate peasantry' and its 'terrible peasant hinterland' would result in the country failing to keep pace with educational and economic progress. He believed Russia was destined to become a place of famine: 'The chances seem altogether against the existence of a great Slavonic power in the world at the beginning of the twenty-first century.' [50]

Again, he was wrong – ironically it was the Soviet Union which attempted to create, by force, the socialist world he craved. Russia today remains an important world power and energy producer. Once more, we see that industrial energy is a better indicator of the social future of a nation than literacy alone.

Surprisingly, Wells forecast the withering away of democracy (as well as the British monarchy) as his anticipated socialist world-state would evolve. He weakly cited democracy's inherent flaws as the main reason for this decline which never happened. [51] Democracy, he argued, would be replaced by a meritocracy, by the power of 'the scientifically educated, disciplined specialist'. [52] To date, democracy has continued to grow globally, not decline. The Arab spring of 2011–2012 illustrates the enduring appeal of democratic principles, however flawed, to peoples of all religions and cultures. Wells was indulging in pre-conceived wish-fulfilment in 'foreseeing' the decline of democracy in the twentieth century. The fallacy of wish-fulfilment is a temptation faced, in different ideological forms, by all futurists.

Neither the British monarchy nor democracy have disappeared as predicted by Wells. Nor did his socialist world-state ever arrive. It can be concluded that *Anticipations* was weak in forecasting future political developments. It is not unusual to get political predictions wrong, perhaps because it is counter-intuitive to make ideologically neutral political forecasts.

Wells was on much more solid ground in predicting technological and social change. The following quote gives the essence of his vision of twentieth-century society: 'We are in the beginning of a new time, with such forces of organisation and unification at work in mechanical traction, in the telephone and telegraph, in a whole wonderland of novel, space-destroying appliances, and in the correlated inevitable advance in practical education, as the world has never felt before.' [53] This would qualify as a substantially true visionary and prescient statement.

He firmly believed that the spread of technology and science, driving social progress, would give momentum to cultural and economic unification through aggregation and assimilation. For example, he predicted that weaker and smaller languages and dialects would gradually disappear with an irresistible gravitation towards the major international languages: 'The Twentieth Century will see the effectual crowding out of most of the weaker languages…French and German will certainly be aggregating languages during the greater portion of the coming years. Of the two I am inclined to think French will spread further than German.' [54]

Wells drew heavily on a Darwinian model of the survival of the fittest/strongest. He correctly understood that Europe would increasingly unite in the twentieth century but he underestimated how much bloodshed and upheaval there would be before that happened, with two catastrophic world wars fought largely between competing European powers. Even now the euro zone is not a federal Europe as he envisaged but an economic union with little political sovereignty surrendered by the participating nations as yet: 'The splendid dream of a Federal Europe…may, perhaps… come to something like realisation at the opening of the twenty-first [century].' [55]

The heart of a united Europe, he predicted, would be a new Rhineland civilisation created by urbanisation and the modernisation of transport and communication. It would be linked by a network of railways and roads. It would form a great urban region from Prague to Paris, whereby different nation-states would be assimilated into one urban culture with French as the dominant language: 'economically, [this region] must become one in the next fifty years. It will almost certainly be the greatest urban region in all the world except that which will arise in the eastern states of North America.' [56] Wells spoke of a 'great synthesis' characterising social development in a motorised world. [57] A massive Francophone, yet multi-lingual, Rhineland economy and society never materialised. However, a euro zone has emerged with an increasingly integrated European economy.

In addition to correctly predicting that ascendancy in world influence would pass from Britain to the US within two to three decades, [58] Wells anticipated a trans-Atlantic market developing between the two powers, alongside his unified Europe. He regarded the emergence of a 'great federation of white, English-speaking peoples', one hundred million strong, with North America as its core, as 'probable'. [59] A cultural and economic trans-Atlantic market between the US and the United Kingdom has, indeed, emerged, with relations between the two nations described by current leaders as a 'special relationship'. In addition, there is the NATO military alliance. However, there is no political federation between the UK and the US. And both countries have become pluralistic, multi-cultural societies, so there is no alliance of 'white, English-speaking peoples' as envisaged by Wells. While he was wrong in predicting linguistic and cultural unification, and about a regional Rhineland society emerging in Europe, he was right that urbanisation and modernisation would create some new economic aggregations, such as we see today in the euro zone, the North American Free Trade Area and the ASEAN bloc (Association of Southeast Asian Nations).

Given his assumptions about scientific progress bringing in its wake aggregation and synthesis of peoples, languages and cultures, Wells wrongly predicted the dissolution of the Jewish identity: 'The Jew will probably lose much of his particularism, intermarry with Gentiles, and cease to be a physically distinct element in human affairs in a century or so.' [60] The opposite has happened – the Jews were given a homeland for the first time in several centuries when the state of Israel was established in 1948. Despite catastrophic losses of life in the Holocaust, the Jewish peoples thrive to this day as a distinct culture throughout the world.

Wells was also wrong that this unification, or aggregation, process would lead ultimately to a 'one world-state at peace with itself'.[61] In *A Modern Utopia* Wells argues that the world state would become the sole landowner, [62] an idea striking the modern democratic citizen as having a distinctly totalitarian bent.

There are some eccentric dimensions to this world-state he foresaw, including the idea that it would be run by an 'informal and open freemasonry' of 'intelligent and quite possibly in some cases wealthy men'.[63] This vision failed to take into account a changing world in which women's rights have become increasingly important.

His theory of a male elite ruling a global government sounds more like an esoteric conspiracy theory than a well-reasoned and plausible political forecast. Other aspects of the vision which seem almost inconceivable today include the ideas of state control of population through eugenics, and the handing over of the guardianship of children to the state: 'The state will…be the reserve guardian of all children' in order to enforce a prescribed kind of parenting.[64] He wanted an 'increasing control of a child's welfare and upbringing by the community'.[65] Wells' prophecy of an elitist, undemocratic, male-dominated world state in total control of society deserved to fail.

Ideology (in this case, an increasingly totalitarian brand of socialism) can cause futuristic blind-spots. Wells underestimated how the forces of nationalism, linguistic pride and capitalism would play out in the twentieth century. Ideology can pollute the scientific basis of forecasts by injecting subjective elements of wish-fulfilment into what should be predictions based purely on facts and causal analysis.

The table that starts on page 26 outlines the record of accuracy of Wells' predictions in *Anticipations*.

Table 2 illustrates that Wells was proficient in technological prognostication, which is the dimension in which he was most comfortable and knowledgeable. This is the area where he made his most important contribution to the scientific study of the future. He added transport to the key drivers established by the pioneers of futures thinking discussed in Chapters 2 and 3, such as knowledge, science, education, population growth, rate of producing the means of subsistence and energy efficiency.

The accuracy of his forecasts per dimension is summarised in table 2.

Prediction	Primary dimension	Accuracy	Theoretical soundness	Theoretical implications
1. Motorisation of transport; new road systems	Technological	Correct ✓	Generally sound; transport systems are economic drivers; neglected role and impact of energy sources for motorisation, i.e. oil	Transportation needs to be linked to its energy sources during foresight production
2. Airplanes to fly before 1950	Technological	Correct ✓ over-estimated timescale	Under-estimated scale of aviation transport revolution	Scale, in time and space, is difficult to predict and needs to be rigorously evaluated
3. Mass diffusion of population to urban suburbs linked to new motorised transit nodes	Social	Correct ✓	Sound	Transport systems seen as a key driver of urban development
4. Decongestion of cities due to suburban diffusion	Social	Incorrect ☒ under-estimated use of high-rise buildings	Partially sound; neglected possible influence of building and architectural trends as well as value of prime land to developers	Take all relevant multi-dimensional factors into account when forecasting large-scale population movements
5. Telephony to revolutionise communication	Technological	Correct ✓	Sound	Communication technologies a key driver of social change
6. Post office to become national provider of economic goods ordered by telephone	Technological	Incorrect ☒ under-estimated role of private sector and over-estimated innovation potential of post office	Partially sound; no fit between new business model of delivery and traditional public service service-provider	Too much influence of ideology on prediction; distribution channels a key aspect of social change

Table 1. Chart of forecasts in H.G. Wells' Anticipations

Prediction	Primary dimension	Accuracy	Theoretical soundness	Theoretical implications
7. Telephone shopping	Technological	Partially correct ✓ foresees shopping from home, but only became possible through internet	Partially sound; under-estimates attraction of in-store shopping as social instinct	Include psychological and cultural dimensions of social trends
8. Moral fragmentation and rise of pluralism	Social	Correct ✓	Sound; education and science led to proliferation of viewpoints; shrinking of world leads to greater diversity	Include role of education as driver of social change
9. Demise of Russia	Political	Incorrect ☒	Over-estimated influence of illiteracy and under-estimated extent to which it can be overcome	Avoid exaggeration of one dimension at expense of other, related dimensions
10. Assimilation of Jews	Social	Incorrect ☒	Under-estimated cultural cohesion of Jewish people; over-estimated forces of unification; ignored history of survival	Include cultural and historical dimensions in social forecasts
11. Trans-Atlantic marketplace between USA and Britain	Economic	Partially correct ✓	Sound; yet over-emphasised cultural grouping and over-estimated political ties	Achieve balance between influences of socio-economic, demographic and political factors

Prediction	Primary dimension	Accuracy	Theoretical soundness	Theoretical implications
12. Withering of democracy	Political	Incorrect ☒	Unsound; under-estimated resilience of democratic systems; superficial analysis of strengths and weaknesses of democracy	Avoid wish-fulfilment in forecasting
13. Withering of monarchy	Political	Incorrect ☒	Unsound; under-estimated constitutional and cultural resilience and history of institution	Include influence of culture and history in social forecasts
14. Rise of French-speaking Rhineland society	Social	Incorrect ☒	Unsound; under-estimated divisive forces of nationalism and resilience of languages	Seek balance of influence of cultural, social, economic and political factors in social forecasts; seek balance of divisive and unifying factors
15. Socialist world-state	Political	Incorrect ☒	Unsound; projection of own ideology; under-estimated capitalism and nationalism as powerful modern shaping forces	Make ideology-agnostic political forecasts based on holistic analysis
16. Federation of Europe	Political	Partially correct; euro zone is economic union with little political union	Partially sound; forces making for unity were foreseen but forces of division were poorly analysed	Political forecasts must be holistic and ideology-agnostic

Dimension	Ratio of successful predictions	Accuracy level	Theoretical soundness	Dimension Ranking
Political	5 predictions: 4 incorrect 1 partially correct = 10% success rate	Very Low	Unsound	4/4
Social	5 predictions: 3 incorrect 2 correct = 40% success rate	Moderate to Low	Inconsistent	3/4
Economic	1 prediction: 1 partially correct = 90% success rate	High	Sound	1/4
Technological	5 predictions: 3 correct 1 partially correct 1 incorrect = 70% success rate	High	Sound	2/4

Table 2. Dimensional accuracy of predictions in *Anticipations*

By analysing the influence of transportation on society, Wells was the first futures thinker to focus attention on the role of technology in determining social development. In the political and sociological fields, his predictions are far less accurate. He seemed to be very poor at forecasting political changes.

There is no doubt that in *Anticipations* Wells showed great flair for prognostication. However, as might be expected from a writer pioneering the trade of futures studies decades before it existed as an academic discipline, the overall forecasting performance is immature, unscientific, theoretically inconsistent and short-sighted, as Tables 1 and 2 show.

Despite these shortcomings, Wells successfully advanced the study of the future. From his vantage point at the start of the twentieth century, he did not know, of course, that Einstein, with his world-changing work on relativity, was about to provide the vital intellectual breakthrough necessary for a science of the future, namely, knowledge of the nature of time.

CHAPTER 5
THE YEAR THE FUTURE ARRIVED

The 1905 publication of Einstein's paper 'On the Electrodynamics of Moving Bodies' in *Annalen der Physik* introduced a radical new approach to physics called relativity theory. Its cornerstone, the concept of space-time, enabled us to understand the physical nature of time, and understanding Einstein's explanation of time in special relativity converted me to belief in the prospect of a genuine science of enquiry into the future. This revelation came after years of believing that the future would always remain unknowable.

Since the future is a phase of time, we need to know what time is in order to understand the future. How can we acquire knowledge of the future if we do not know what it is? The prevailing conception of time in physics, in my view, becomes the theoretical keystone of futurology. Einstein showed that time is not some sort of clock in the sky that ticks at the same rate for everyone. It still comes as a surprise to me every time I am reminded that time is neither universal nor separate from space.

The man chosen in December 1999 as *Time* magazine's Person of the Century wrote in his 1916 book *Relativity*: 'there is no more commonplace statement than that the world in which we live is a four-dimensional space-time continuum.' [66] This deceptively simple sentence, written by the great man with a tinge of irony, is perhaps the most revolutionary scientific statement ever made.

In the history of science, the notion of a four-dimensional world is equivalent in its world-changing impact to the Copernican Revolution which dethroned earth from its fixed, central position in the solar system. Space-time, and other aspects of the theory of relativity, corrected aspects of the Newtonian worldview which had prevailed for more than two centuries (218 years, to be exact).

What does it mean to live in this four-dimensional world of space-time identified by Einstein?

Einstein pictured space itself as a three-dimensional continuum because 'it is possible to describe the position of a point (at rest) by means of three numbers (coordinates) x,y,z'. [67] The number of coordinates by which an object may be measured determines how many dimensions it has at its position in space. For example, the surface of the earth is two dimensional, encompassing longitude and latitude, but when one adds height above sea level, a third dimension is introduced.

In *Why does E=mc²?* Cox and Forshaw refer to this 3-D space as a kind of giant box containing all the objects in the universe, including us.[68] Special relativity added a fourth value, time, to space's three coordinates to form a 4-D continuum. We exist in this 4-D space-time. [69]

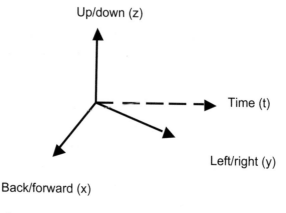

Figure 3. Fourth dimension of time (t) added to three space dimensions (x,y,z)

In Figure 3, time is a core coordinate used to measure motions and positions of objects in space: 'An event, wherever it has taken place, would be fixed in space…by the three perpendiculars, *x,y,z* on the coordinate planes, and with regard to time by a time value *t*'. [70]

Let us suppose for a moment that you or I are the object being measured with these four coordinates. This experience could be visualised as a person inside a time 'bubble' further located within a 3-D space 'box'.

Throughout our lives we are moving organisms within a 4-D reality where we have four potential directions, namely, up/down, right/left, forwards/backwards and *motion in time* as shown in figure 3. Einstein refers to these coordinates several times as magnitudes,[71] or measurements of important dimensions, which can be expressed in numerical values. He argued that the time coordinate 'plays exactly the same role as the three space coordinates'. [72] Space-time is a fusion of time and three-dimensional space.

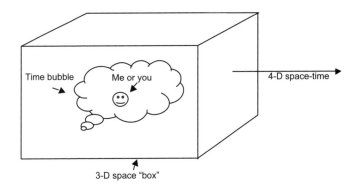

Figure 4. Living in four-dimensional space-time

Hawking describes space-time as follows: 'time and space are intertwined. It is something like adding a fourth direction of future/past to the usual left/right, forward/backward, and up/down....In space-time, time is no longer separate from the three dimensions of space.' [73]

He characterises the past as the 'backward' direction of time and the future as its 'forward' direction. Our motion through time is just as real and just as important as our motion through space. It is interesting that some peoples of the Canadian First Nations, for example, use language to express time as a form of distance, describing an elder as having 'covered a long distance'. [74]

Through his theoretical marriage of space and time, Einstein, in effect, spatialised time. He embedded time within space. The demystification and spatialisation of time in space-time he brought about is good news for futurology. Suddenly time – including the future – is no longer an unknowable mystery. The way has been opened to gain scientific knowledge of the future. Since we already know a great deal about the spatial world in which we live, including the laws and principles by which it operates, we can better understand how time works as an extension of space in its role as part of space-time. The spatialisation of time enables us to build far clearer pictures of time's behaviour. In turn, this gives insight into how the future works.

Prior to special relativity, the prevailing model of physics was Newtonian mechanics. It was based primarily on three laws of motion formulated in 1687 [75] Newton viewed time as 'fixed and absolute, the same for all observers, and distinct from space'. [76] He once declared: 'The flow of absolute time cannot be changed.'[77] The great scientist depicted a world of absolute unchanging time and absolute space in which all motion worked precisely and predictably according to the laws of motion.[78] The physical world in his world view was conceived as functioning more or less like clockwork.

However, in 1905, special relativity demonstrated that Newton's concept of absolute time was wrong: 'In the theory of relativity there is no unique, absolute time, but, instead, each individual has his own personal measure of time that depends on where he is and how he is moving.'[79] Absolute time – 'meaning a time that…tick-tocks along independent of any observations of it'[80] – was no longer seen as real since it could not be observed or measured as such by every observer.

As a consequence Newton's clockwork universe was replaced as the governing worldview of science by Einstein's more counter-intuitive, dynamic space-time world. In it, everything is relative to everything else except that its one cosmic constant is the speed of light. This has a blindingly fast and absolute speed of 299,792,458 metres per second.[81] It was not time that was absolute in the universe, it was the speed of light.

Einstein discovered that, with the exception of light, all measurements of time and space, as well as events, are relative to the reference point from which they are observed. The word 'relative' here is opposite to words like 'absolute', 'universal' and 'invariant'. The latter word means 'quantities that everybody can agree on regardless of their frame of reference'.[82] 'Relative', by contrast, may be defined as: dependent upon changing frames of reference, where measurements of an object or event vary quite literally according to the vantage point from where they are viewed. For example, the event of a train passing an observer on an embankment would be perceived and measured differently by a passenger on the moving train.[83]

Einstein used this well-known example of the moving train in relation to an embankment to illustrate that motion is relative to the point of reference from which measurements of aspects of objects, such as speed, direction, etc., are made. Measurements of time and distance, too, vary according to where the observer is placed and whether he/she is at rest or in motion. This idea of the non-universality of measurements of time and distance constitutes the 'relativity' within relativity theory.

In relativity theory, time is *not* the same for every person or object in all positions and at all speeds, even though we instinctively sense it *should* be: 'according to classical mechanics, time is absolute, i.e. it is independent of the position and condition of motion of the system of coordinates…in the theory of relativity…time is robbed of its independence'. [84]

To arrive at his relativistic understanding of time, Einstein conducted thought experiments involving stationary and moving clocks. He concluded that clocks in motion must move ('tick') more slowly than stationary clocks because the light emitted by the moving clock has further to travel than the light emitted by a stationary clock. The light in both cases travels at exactly the same speed, being absolute. For a clock in motion, the ticks literally take longer. Time measured by the moving clock becomes marginally slower than would be the case for a stationary clock.

If time slows down, or changes, when objects are travelling at speed, it cannot be a process or phenomenon which is independent from space in any meaningful sense. And it is not only speed that changes the actual rate of time. Gravitational mass also alters time's rate: 'The stronger the field, the greater the effect (which is known as "gravitational time dilation").' [85] Gravitational time dilation happens on earth and out in the planetary spheres. On earth, the time dilation effect is miniscule but real nonetheless. Close to black holes, however, *time slows down almost to a complete stop*: 'suppose that identical twins spend the night in bunk beds. One sleeps a metre above the other. The next morning, the twin who slept in the top bunk is a few trillionths of a second older….Close to a black hole, clocks run far slower than in empty space. Near the event horizon, the effective surface of the black hole, clocks come almost to a complete stop.' [86] A black hole's gravity causes extreme time dilation. This example dramatically demonstrates there is no such thing as absolute 'one time for all'.

The same force that distorts the rate of time also warps space, strongly curving it. [87] Objects, for example, quite literally shrink at high speeds. [88] Moving objects have been shown to shrink along the direction of their motion in an extraordinary phenomenon known as the Fitzgerald contraction: [89] 'Having accepted the fact moving clocks run slower than stationary ones, we are forced to conclude that moving sticks are shorter than stationary ones'. [90] Welcome to our wonderful world in which a clock in motion ticks slower than a stationary one and a stick will start to get shorter at great speeds. We want to focus on the nature and behaviour of time because we want to understand the future better.

Time, we have seen, is relative. This fact about time is often illustrated by the fascinating twins paradox. This is a thought-experiment whereby one twin is imagined to travel in a high-speed rocket close to the speed of light for several years (see Figure 5 below). When this space-travelling twin returns to earth, he/she will literally be a younger person than the earth-bound twin: 'If one twin goes to a star three light years away in a super rocket that travels at ⅗ the speed of light, the journeys out and back take five years in the frame of the earth…but the twin on the rocket will age only four years on the outward journey, and another four years on the return journey. When she gets back home, she will be two years younger than her stay-at-home sister, who has aged the full ten years.' [91]

This example seems like science fiction but it is based on scientific fact. It shows decisively that the nature of time is altered by spatial factors like speed. In Figure 5, the fast-moving twin enjoys a slower rate of time than her earth-bound sister so stays younger longer.

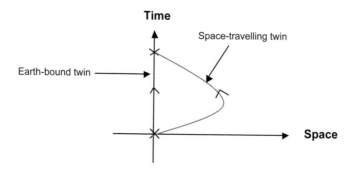

Figure 5. Illustration of the twins paradox

Einstein's model of space and time has been described as 'the foundation on which all of modern physics rests'. [92] Yet the theory has not been fully absorbed by most people as part of our way of experiencing the world, largely because its concepts are disconcertingly counterintuitive. [93]

The fact that Einstein's well-proven theory of time is highly abstract may be one of the main reasons why humanity, outside the realm of physics, has not yet taken on board the implications of his extraordinary conceptual discoveries. Certainly the study of the future has not yet embraced the far-reaching implications of his relativist conception of time.

As odd as Einstein's marriage of space and time may at first glance appear to be, this theory happens to hold the key to advancing human knowledge to the next level, that is, by knowing and planning for the future.

The metaphor of a marriage between space and time is descriptive of a very close relationship. It is important to grasp just how closely intertwined space and time really are.

'Continuum' is defined as a continuous sequence, [94] that is, one which forms an indivisible whole. Use of the compound noun 'space-time' was necessitated by the principles of Einstein (and before him, of Minkowski). [95] Space-time conjoined two pre-existing words, retrospectively creating a new compound noun, representing, at the time of its coinage, a new concept. For centuries space and time were separate words and concepts. [96] Subsequent to the coinage of the term space-time it has proven very difficult for people to accept it or even to conceive of it.

Yet, our commonplace understanding of time as independent of space, and universal in nature, is factually wrong. There is never going to be a universal 'one time for all' on earth. Time is not located above or beyond space. There is no clock in the sky.

I have suggested that time and space are not just loosely connected. Rather they are wedded in holy matrimony throughout the cosmos: 'Space and time can be merged into a single entity that we call "space-time" and distances in space-time are invariant.' [97]

The intimate connection between them is shown in the law referred to at the end of this quote. What does it mean that distances in space-time are constant and invariant? Basically it means that if an object is travelling fast through space its 'speed' through time will slow down correspondingly so that its total amount of space and time 'distance' remains exactly the same. We saw this amazing principle at work in the moving clocks which ticked slower than the stationary ones, and also in the twins paradox whereby the earth-bound twin did not travel fast through space and so went through time faster than the space-borne twin who consequently aged less. Greene (2004) explains that the combined speed of any object's motion through space and its motion through time is always precisely equal to the speed of light. [98] He calls the combined motion through time and space *light-speed* motion: 'The key fact, Einstein discovered, is that these two kinds of motion are always complementary.' [99]

I share this peculiar feature of space-time to indicate just how close the relationship is between space and time. Cox and Forshaw define 'space-time distance' as a factor of distance travelled and time taken to travel, all relative to the speed of light. It is a law that everything moves through space-time at the same speed. By this is meant every object in motion has the same 'fixed quota' of space-time speed – if an object travels faster in space, it will correspondingly 'travel' slower in time. [100] This is a mind-boggling feature of physical existence.

When a clock is moving through space, it has correspondingly less of its 'space-time quota' left over for motion through time: 'a moving clock doesn't move as fast through time as a stationary one, which is just another way of saying that it ticks more slowly. In contrast, a clock sitting at rest whizzes along in the time direction at the speed of c [speed of light] with no motion in space. It therefore ticks along as fast as possible'. [101] It is remarkable that a person asleep and motionless on a bed is still moving through space-time – since he or she is ageing, that is, moving through time. The same goes for a parked car. The vehicle is moving through space-time while standing stock-still in its parking space. These examples prove how dynamic the 4-D world we live in really is.

This indivisible space-time continuum is dynamic in that both time and space change when an object is in motion at speeds which are high enough to affect the magnitude of some of their dimensions. The fabric of space-time, within our expanding universe, can dilate and shrink like stretched canvas. There is an 'ever continuing expansion of the background space-time of the universe'. [102]

Within this intimate space-time entity, time behaves according to scientific principles. That is one of the reasons I am excited as a futurist about getting to know time better. Its unknowability has been stripped away. Time has been demystified by physics.

Hawking uses the evocative phrase 'the arrow of time' to describe the idea that time is a direction moving away from the past into the future like an arrow fired forwards. As futurist Wendell Bell has stated: 'We are constantly moving with the arrow of time on a one-way trip out of the past in an on-going present toward the future.' [103]

If Einstein discovered a new physics of time, which proves fundamental to the possibility of knowledge of the future, it is Stephen Hawking who has best explained the meaning of physical time to a modern audience. He has deepened our understanding of time, showing it is a profound dimension of the 4-D world we all live in.

CHAPTER 6
THREE ARROWS OF TIME

Hawking distinguishes between three arrows of time: 'First, there is the thermodynamic arrow of time, the direction of time in which disorder or entropy increases. Then there is the psychological arrow of time. This is the direction in which we feel time passes, the direction in which we remember the past but not the future. Finally, there is the cosmological arrow of time. This is the direction of time in which the universe is expanding rather than contracting.'[104]

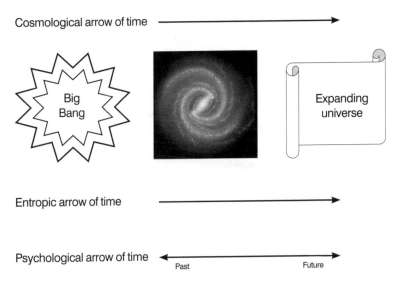

Figure 6. Hawking's three arrows of time

In cosmological time, the universe continues to expand at a rapid rate,[105] reinforcing the fact that the physical world, the whole of space-time, is in constant motion as it spreads out across tracts of outer space. The birth of time itself has been described in cosmological terms: 'Our expanding universe is not infinitely old, but rather has a definite age. If we start with the expansion of the universe as observed today, and then "run the clock backward" to extrapolate the motion to earlier times, all of the matter in the universe reaches an infinite density at a given time in the past. This singular point represents the Big Bang itself, which defines the beginning of time.' [106] The Big Bang was born out of a 'foamy region of high-energy space-time'. [107] Since then the universe has expanded into more diffused, lower-order states.

Space-time was born as one at the Big Bang. Cosmological time, the first arrow in Figure 6, has existed for about 13.7 billion years, the estimated age of the universe. Time is a physical dimension in which all existence evolves, moves, changes and lives across a truly vast cosmic timeline. [108]

Entropic time [109] is the tendency for increased disorder in the world as expressed in the second law of thermodynamics. Hawking explains entropy using an analogy: 'there are always many more disordered states than…ordered ones. For example, consider the pieces of a jigsaw in a box. There is one, and only one, arrangement in which the pieces make a complete picture…there are a very large number of arrangements in which the pieces are disordered'. [110]

Since there are many more possible disordered states than there are ordered ones, it is more probable that disorder will increase with time, especially when the system in question starts off in a relative condition of order. In other words, there is a built-in tendency for physical systems to move into more disorganised conditions. [111] In more disorganised states, there is a dissolution of structure, a diffusion into greater homogeneity, or co-mingled sameness. This is an important tendency of the physical world to bear in mind when looking ahead to the future.

Entropy is an integral part of time's behaviour. It is, in fact, ubiquitous, from the evaporation of black holes far out in outer space to the way a fire burns down at a family barbecue: 'the same Second Law operative here on earth appears to hold everywhere in the observable universe to distances far beyond those of any relevance to local conditions, such as in galaxies thousands of millions of light years distant, to times far earlier than the beginnings of life on earth'. [112] The effects of entropy need to be accounted for in all future outlooks.

Left to run their course, systems in nature and in society will tend to dissipate energy and order 'toward a lukewarm uniformity'. [113] Order, on the whole, is fleeting. [114] Entropy, described as the degree of disorder in a system, will naturally increase if things are left to their own devices, without interventions. As a consequence of this universal law, it is vital to create order out of disorder to counteract entropy's dissolution of structures and systems. This entails managing the effort and energy required to maintain order. If we wish to become future-facing beings we need to plan well ahead to create the foundations of order in the future.

Penrose describes entropy as the measure of a system's disorder or randomness: 'things are getting more "random" all the time. So if we set up a particular situation, and then let the dynamics evolve it into the future, the system will evolve into a more random-looking state as time progresses… according to the Second Law, things are getting progressively more and more random with time, but that this represents merely an overwhelming probability, not quite an absolute certainty'. [115]

Penrose uses the word 'disorganized' as a synonym for 'random'. Just as the heat of a fire dissipates its energy over a larger volume of particles in the air, leading to the gradual cooling down of the fire, so systems in nature and society tend to lose their cohesion and structure, or inner order, over time as their energy is used up. Carroll (2011) describes entropy as energy which has become useless after having been dissipated. [116]

The tendency for energy to become dissipated in the physical world, especially in closed systems, and for order to decrease over time, is mirrored in other dimensions. Not only do gardens lose their shape when left unattended, but organisations, from family households to large corporations, also tend to become chaotic when management rules and practices, or the system of governance, break down. [117] Entropy may be understood in this non-technical sense as a dissolution of structure over time in the absence of strategic human intervention.

Just as the laws of causation posit the existence of a future in which effects take place, so the law describing entropy assumes the existence of the future. In fundamental ways, the future, in physics, inheres in the present as a consequence of nature's laws. The present time in physics, that is, is always 'pregnant' with the future. The future is immanent, or in-dwelling, in the present. As an ultrasound scan of a baby in the womb reveals its shape, sex and general health, so forecasts can scan a future already existing in the womb of the present.

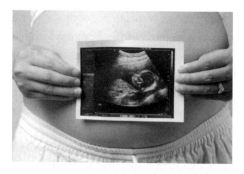

Figure 7. The present is 'pregnant' with the future

Nature points to the future when its laws will produce their effects. Both cosmological time and entropic time for Hawking move inexorably into the future, as Figure 6 illustrates. Our universe, with its space-time fabric, points squarely in the direction of the future. Our world is like a gigantic ship always facing in the direction of its destination. This fact alone should inspire us to live for the future, to be orientated towards what is yet to come. This would represent a powerful philosophical shift, preparing the way for a permanently proactive mind-set.

What else do the cosmological and entropic characteristics of time tell the futurist? Time is evolutionary. Systems evolve *into* the future. As Penrose says, they have a 'time-evolution'. By studying past evolution cycles of systems and then taking into account the influences of various laws of nature, futurists can predict future evolutions of a system.

It is interesting to note as pointed out by Penrose that the Second Law does not work in reverse. Once again, we see existence has a built-in bias to the future. This feature is perhaps the most striking aspect of the behaviour of time.

Before discussing psychological time, Hawking's third arrow, it is important to grasp the relation between cosmic and entropic kinds of time. As the universe expands and cools in cosmological time, according to the Big Bang theory, 'radiation is stretched out to lower energy…'. [118] This explains the tendency in entropy to dissipate into lower energy, lower-order states through an on-going spreading out of energy across more space. Furthermore, Hawking explains why the entropic, or thermodynamic, arrow and the cosmological arrow point in the same direction. The latter arrow he considers necessary for intelligent life to exist [119] as conditions for life could not exist in a contracting universe.[120] So the expanding universe provides the cosmological preconditions for intelligent life to exist and to move to lower-order states from the initial high order state of the Big Bang. Since the latter is understood to have been of 'extraordinarily low entropy', [121] the overall entropy of the universe vastly increases over cosmic time. [122]

An expanding universe pictures the whole space-time world in constant motion, subject to endless change in position. An entropic universe pictures a world tending towards increased disorder, with total net energy staying constant, according to the laws of thermodynamics, but spread out over a greater area and therefore more dissipated. In physics, time is not a conductor of order, but a conveyor belt of high-rates of change and pressures towards inherent "entropic" disorder. This is a key point for understanding the future. It is another startling characteristic of time.

Both cosmological and entropic time are unidirectional. That is, they both only move towards the future. Physics shows that nature's normal time direction is future-facing. Space, by contrast, does not seem to have a direction as such. We can go in whichever direction we choose. Psychological time is the only form of time, in Figure 6, which is bi-directional. Psychological, or human, time is able to move backwards through memory: the reconstruction of the past. It is also able to move forwards to anticipate the future based on past experience. Both the past direction and future direction of psychological time are performed by the same part of the brain. This is known as mental time travel and is regarded by psychologists as a critical tool of human survival and of mastery of the environment. The brain can reconstruct the past and preconstruct the future.

It is the quality of human memory in this tripartite model of time which must play the role of agent of order, a stabilising and balancing force. In many ways mental time travel is a key to human civilisation. It is also essential for the creation of order from disorder. What this means is that human systems have the opportunity to be self-correcting, to learn from errors and to apply rationality in the pursuit of order at the expense of natural entropy. Memory works in the opposite direction to entropic time and has been shown to be crucial for planning for, and simulating, the future. The brain processes memories as well as anticipatory 'memories of the future'.

While Einstein and Hawking unlocked a new world of space-time with brilliant thinking about physical time, the discipline of futures studies has not worked out the significance of Einstein's theory of space-time for studying the future. The future may have arrived in 1905, the year of the discovery of the special theory of relativity, but, sadly, the twentieth century did not develop a science of the future. Meanwhile, we are running out of time to solve major current global problems, like climate change, Peak Oil and environmental degradation. We need to accelerate our understanding and use of the future before it is too late, and these problems, exacerbated by a lack of long-term planning, reach their respective tipping-points and plunge us into an irreversible global decline.

The physics of time attaches a radical value of urgency to the future. It also provides a deep understanding of time, opening a door into the future.

CHAPTER 7
ON THE FRONTIER OF THE FUTURE

1905 should have been the breakthrough year for a science of the future thanks to the brilliance of Einstein. However, its development was delayed for much of the century, although the study of the future as an academic discipline did take shape in the second half of the century. The following five factors appear to have created this hiatus in establishing this new field of scientific study.

Firstly, the abstract, counter-intuitive concepts of relativity theory, including the notion of space-time, may have hindered their acceptance into mainstream thought and culture.

Secondly, two world wars followed this time of intense intellectual discovery. A protracted period of wars produced a more pessimistic mood about progress and the future.

Thirdly, the worldview of post-modernism, building on this *zeitgeist* of pessimism, created a widespread intellectual climate of antipathy towards science, rationality and order. Post-modernism has exerted a dominant influence on culture and thought, especially since the 1960s and 1970s. Bell notes that the theory of futures studies developed at a time when the positivist theory of knowledge and science itself was under attack from post-modernist thinking and an intellectual bias against science was evolving. [123] Ironically, at this very time the world was lurching towards major global problems for which scientific knowledge offer potential solutions.

Fourthly, the study of the future in the second half of the century largely coalesced around the standpoint articulated by French futurist Bertrand de Jouvenel that futures thinking is an art rather than a science. His classic text *The Art of Conjecture*, published in 1967, influenced a whole generation of futurists into accepting the inscrutability of the future. An odd situation arose in which futurists were compelled to study a phenomenon they did not believe was real. The discipline became an increasingly speculative field of thought. De Jouvenel's work, however, glossed over some historic achievements in accurate predictions of the social future. It also overlooked the implications of Einstein's theory of space-time for the study of the future.

Fifthly, the role of the uncertainty principle in quantum mechanics has had a negative influence on futures thinking, reinforcing the idea of the future as a domain of uncertainty. Yet quantum mechanics has little bearing on the world of special relativity or on its core concept of space-time (see Appendix 3). Nor do the minuscule particles of quantum mechanics have a strong ontological influence on the large-scale macroscopic world you and I live in. It is this macroscopic realm which is the domain of futurology and all of the social sciences.

Largely as a result of these five factors, attempts to create a mature social science of the future floundered after H.G. Wells. 1905 should have kick-started an intellectual revolution in knowledge about the future. Fortunately, it may not be too late to create an alternative trajectory for a study of the future, this time as a science, not as an art.

Apparently unbeknownst to de Jouvenel, an American geophysicist working in the field of industrial energy, M. King Hubbert (1903–1989), had made some major predictions in 1956 on the scale of those made by W. Stanley Jevons almost a century earlier.

While Jevons had forecast the decline of British global dominance due to decreasing domestic supplies of coal, Hubbert accurately foresaw the peak of both US and global oil production. In the process, he became the father of the theory of Peak Oil. This phenomenon has far-reaching worldwide implications for our own times. It could become the biggest change in industrial history, a turning-point in the evolution of human society.

In his prognostic paper 'Nuclear Energy and the Fossil Fuels' presented to the American Petroleum Institute in San Antonio, Texas, in March 1956, Hubbert, then employed by Shell, correctly predicted that US oil production would peak within twenty years by the early 1970s. In the paper, he also forecast that global oil production would peak at the turn of the century. Hubbert's 1956 forecasts show that scientific principles can be applied to studies of the social future, flying in the face of the idea, postulated by de Jouvenel, that forecasts are a matter of conjecture, not of science.

Hubbert argued that supplies of fossil fuels like oil accumulated over millions of years of geological history. Fossil fuels represent highly 'concentrated power'. This power led to what he termed the increase in the immensity of human operations by several orders of magnitude. Since no significant new fossil fuels would be created in the following millennia, earth's current supplies were effectively finite. Such a fixed supply, he stated, would be progressively exhausted over time.

The geophysicist then looked at global annual production figures for coal, oil and gas. He noticed that progress in production followed the same curve pattern for all three fuel types. The upward curve began slowly and then gathered speed until the highest point was reached after which it curved downwards in a typical bell curve (see Figure 8 below). Initial rates of production increase exponentially until physical limits permanently put an end to these rates of growth. After the production peak, growth declines towards zero.

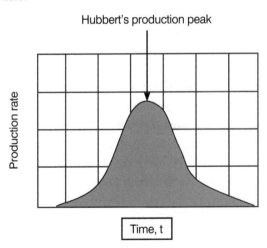

Figure 8. Hubbert's bell-shaped cycle of production of exhaustible resources
(Shaded area = ultimate cumulative production)

The symmetrical bell shape in Figure 8, representing the lifespan of production of any finite resource, is a sobering graphic. In particular, there is a sharp fall in production after the peak is reached, a mirror image of the rate of exponential growth prior to peak. In this case, a period of steep decline is the flip side of high growth. Turbulence may result as production cycles turn downwards once peaks, or inflection points, are reached.

The pattern in the graph represents an underlying economic cycle which underpins industrial energy, shown in chapter 3 to be a driver of social progress. It is patterns like these that led me to describe study of the future as a form of pattern recognition across developmental timelines.

Turning to oil, Hubbert showed that between the point when production began in America in 1859 and the end of 1955, 53 billion barrels had been produced. The first half of this amount took eighty years, from 1859 to 1939, to produce. The second half took only sixteen years, a remarkable acceleration in production. This represents the exponential growth leading to peak in the bell-shaped cycle. Sadly, such acceleration is later bound to be mirrored by a rapid decrease after peak.

Hubbert based his accurate forecast on what he termed the best possible estimates of the ultimate reserves, or fixed supply, of oil. He estimated the total potential oil reserves of the United States to be 150–200 billion barrels. At the time of the presentation, 52.5 billion barrels had been extracted, leaving 97.5 billion barrels still to be produced. By extrapolating expected production rates, Hubbert could estimate the future production curve for US petroleum. He forecast that the production peak would occur around 1970, with total exhaustion of the resource taking place around 2050. As Hubbert predicted, US oil production peaked at 10,200,000 barrels per day (1,620,000 m3/d) in 1970–71. This is one of the greatest predictions of all time.

US oil production has been in decline ever since, with dire consequences: 'Since its 1970 oil peak, the US suffered a slow but inexorable economic decline. Formerly the world's foremost creditor nation, it has become by far the world's foremost debtor nation...recent US history is marked by increasing energy dependency and decreasing solvency.' [124]

At the time Hubbert made this prediction, the US was the world's leading oil producer and exporter. It was the most explored region on earth for petroleum. Back in 1956 a mere handful of individuals would have been able to foresee this great turning-point. It was going to mean the beginning of the end for America's oil-based era of prosperity, which had turned it into the world's greatest superpower.

Hubbert employed the same methodology to forecast the peak of world oil production, known as Peak Oil. Based on initial reserves of 1250 billion barrels and on annual production rates, he calculated the production peak for world oil was likely to happen around 2000. [125]

He based his production forecasts on accurate data, beginning in the right way by drawing up an inventory of energy supplies. 'On the basis of the present estimates of the ultimate reserves of petroleum and natural gas, it appears that the culmination of world production of these products should occur within about half a century, while the culmination for petroleum and natural gas in both the United States and the state of Texas should occur within the next few decades.' [126] Time has proved these words to be accurate.

Towards the end of his paper, Hubbert forecast that nuclear power would replace fossil fuels as the greatest industrial energy source. He predicted a new nuclear era for the world, given the high energy content of uranium. [127] He devised an impressive 10,000-year time scale in which to frame his energy forecasts, which he called, humbly, 'the time perspective'. The era of fossil fuels would be measured in a few short centuries, whereas nuclear power, he believed, would dwarf their contribution in the long-run and dominate industry for thousands of years.

Hubbert correctly envisaged the rise of nuclear power. Yet, he overestimated its rate of growth. This was largely because he was unaware of the disastrous social impacts of nuclear accidents that lay ahead like the ones at Three Mile Island in 1979 and the Chernobyl Nuclear Power Plant in Ukraine in 1986.

Even scientifically formulated predictions can be wrong if unforeseen factors, in this case the health and environmental risks involved in nuclear power, are overlooked. Hubbert did not realise at the time that nuclear power was a different kind of energy with a radically new risk profile. Nevertheless, his underlying theory that uranium has a high energy content with huge potential industrial application remains sound, as can be seen by the current worldwide revival in nuclear power plant production in developing and developed nations.

His faith in the ability of nuclear power to replace the role of fossil fuels gave him grounds for an optimistic conclusion to his historic presentation in which he speculated humanity may have found an energy supply adequate for its needs for several centuries.

Unfortunately, this optimism turned out to have been unfounded. In addition, his absolute faith in nuclear power probably led to an underestimation of the long-term future of renewable energy.

Nevertheless, his 1956 paper contains highly accurate scientific foresight with implications for society right up to the present time.

In my view, Hubbert's work is one the greatest pieces of social foreknowledge ever produced. But Hubbert was a geologist, not a futurist. He did not attempt to systematically draw out the implications of the coming oil depletion crisis for the future of society as a whole. It is only now, through the work of groups like the Association of Peak Oil, the Post-Carbon Institute and the Oil Depletion Analysis Centre (ODAC), that the potentially disastrous consequences of Peak Oil for industry and society are becoming better understood.

A science of the future, had it existed in the second half of the century, could have taken Hubbert's 1956 energy forecasts and constructed models for dealing with the oil depletion crisis they foretold. This would have provided humanity with a few more valuable decades to prepare for what is likely to become one of the biggest economic and social transitions to a new energy order ever undertaken.

Instead, de Jouvenel's concerns about the future as a fit subject for scientific study became entrenched. In turn, this may have led to more idealistic, broad-based formulations of the purpose of studying the future, such as: 'the goals of futurists are to contribute toward making the world a better place in which to live, benefitting people and the life-sustaining capacities of the Earth'. [128] Futurist Wendell Bell, for example, proposed a nine-fold schema of purposes for futures studies:

1. The study of possible futures

2. The study of probable futures

3. The study of images of the future

4. The study of the knowledge foundations of futures studies

5. The study of the ethical foundations of futures studies

6. Interpreting the past and orientating the present

7. Integrating knowledge and values for designing social action

8. Increasing democratic participation in imaging and designing the future

9. Communicating and advocating a particular image of the future. [129]

Greater clarity and focus could be gained for the discipline by replacing such a multiplicity of aims with the single goal of carrying out a scientific study of the future. Period. In addition, a science of the future would be better understood by the world than a more speculative future studies programme. In view of the underlying theoretical problem of not having a thorough conceptual understanding of what the future – or time for that matter – is, the oft-stated claim that futures studies aims 'to discover or invent, examine and evaluate, and propose possible, probable and preferable futures' has worn thin over time. [130]

A science of the future has not yet been created. Since futures studies has not developed a theory of time, derived from physics, there is no ontology or epistemology of the future which can explain how the future can be known using scientific methods.

This has led to a current crisis within our field. Wendell Bell admits that epistemology remains 'one of the least developed aspects of futures studies'. [131] He acknowledges that there has been a failure to define the philosophical bases of assertions about the future: 'the major issues of the nature of the knowledge in the futures field – as apart from the mechanics of specific methods – have received relatively little sustained attention and critical thought'. [132]

As a result of this lack of a basic epistemology or ontology of time, Bell argues that 'the present status of futures studies may be precarious and its future as a separate and distinct field may fail to materialize as fully as some futurists believe'. [133] I do not share this pessimism about the future of futures studies. It can reinvent itself as futurology, based on scientific principles.

Furthermore, there is no sustained theoretical discussion on the nature of time by the contributing futurists in the five volumes of the *Knowledge Base of Futures Studies (professional edition)*. Many of them appear to subscribe, directly or indirectly, to the principle of Bertrand de Jouvenel that futures studies is more of an art than a science [134] due to the inherent 'unknowability' of the future as a domain of uncertainty. The term 'space-time' does not appear in the Glossary of this international futures studies knowledge base. Nor is the concept discussed in the two volumes of *Foundations of Futures Studies* (2003 edition).

Bell identifies de Jouvenel's work as a key text in the development of modern futures studies, [135] agreeing that 'the future is non-evidential and cannot be observed; therefore there are no facts about the future'. [136] This is a common argument within the discipline of futures studies. Since the future does not yet exist, this line of reasoning argues, it is a non-factual phenomenon. The theory of space-time, however, provides persuasive theoretical grounds for revising this line of thought, as Chapter 8 will now make clear.

Whilst there is undoubtedly an impressive and fascinating global knowledge base of futures studies which is strategically useful for policymakers and business leaders, it appears to be built on a comparatively weak theoretical foundation.

The way to overcome this crisis in futures thinking is to develop an epistemology of the future based on an ontology of time. But first, let us revisit the theory of time as expounded by contemporary physics to better understand time's features and behaviour. A scientific understanding of the concept of the future will provide a foundation for our model for producing foreknowledge.

CHAPTER 8
A SCIENCE OF TIME

It is interesting that no academic discipline 'owns' or claims time as its specialised subject-matter. This is because time is fundamental to the whole of human existence. Would philosophy, religion or history, for example, be more appropriate than physics to oversee the study of time on behalf of civilisation? Since time, like space, has been around for over 13 billion years, it is clearly a cosmic medium in which all existence evolves. More specifically, special relativity has demonstrated that time is the fourth dimension of the 4-D world of space-time inside which we live.

Einstein's doctrine of space-time has demystified time, stripping away some of its intangibility or mysteriousness. Hawking's A *Brief History of Time* has rendered time more accessible to conceptual analysis. And cosmology has illuminated key characteristics of time, such as its production of high rates of change and disorder.

Of all academic disciplines, physics, in general, and cosmology, in particular, have revealed the most about the nature of time. It would therefore seem appropriate for these branches of science to continue to shepherd our knowledge of time. Social sciences like history, sociology and philosophy, as well as theology and religion, can provide insights about behaviour of social phenomena over time to build upon what could be called the physics of time.

Physics shows that future time has a special status as the most important phase of time. For one, it is the time in which scientific laws are fulfilled and scientific predictions tested. Multiple effects happen in a future time relative to their antecedent causes. And we have seen that entropic and cosmological time both direct existence irreversibly towards the future. Neither causation nor entropy happen in reverse. Their processes are future-facing. In this light, it is hardly surprising that empiricist philosopher Bertrand Russell, one of the greatest minds of the last century, stated that the future (and the past) 'are as real as the present'.[137]

Time is the cosmic evolutionary medium. Science shows everything is evolving, including the universe. The space-time we see around us at any given time is an evolving entity. It is a living product of past-evolution analogous to a child being a living product of its parents. Present time is like a bridge between past time which has vanished, leaving traces, and future time which fulfills the evolutionary process. So time always faces the future, away from the past. The momentum of time constantly spills over into the future like waves on a shore. This invites humans to be proactive, better aligned to the nature of time, harnessing its evolutionary momentum. Being proactive, in turn, will elevate consciousness to a higher level.

By demystifying and 'spatialising' time, the space-time theory has opened the gate for a science of the future. Significant attributes of time have been illuminated in Einstein's theory of relativity and Hawking's doctrine of the three arrows of time.

These characteristics can be expressed in ten core propositions about time.

1. Time is embedded within 4-D space-time
Time is a cosmic medium which has no independent existence outside of space; it is an integral part of the space-time fabric of the universe born at the Big Bang. This means time is spatialised, subject in its very nature to spatial factors like motion and gravity. It is not 'out there' but is here with us as an intimate part of everyday spatial existence.

2. Time measures motion and direction of entities through space-time
Time is an important measurement of any object's position and motion through space-time.

3. Time is relative (i.e. non-universal)
This means it is measurable only from specific frames of reference. It varies according to these different frames of reference. There is no 'clock in the sky'.

4. Entropic time is the time in which disorder tends to increase
The Second Law of Thermodynamics shows there are many more disordered states for systems than ordered ones and that there is therefore a probability of greater degrees of disorder in future, especially when systems are in an initial state of order.

5. Cosmological time is the time created by an expanding universe
Intelligent life could not be sustained in a contracting universe. A rapidly

expanding universe keeps everything in constant motion, which, in turn, enables life, with all is lifecycles, to exist.

6. Time is future-facing
Since cosmological and entropic time are uni-directional and irreversible, the overwhelming direction of time is towards the future. In the physical world, time is rushing towards the future. There is an undeniable urgency and importance about time, given its irreversibility. (If we go in the wrong direction in space we can correct our mistake; if we embark on a dodgy course of action, the consequences over time will be irretrievable.)

7. Time has continuity, with the future immanent in the present
The principle of continuity ensures that time flows from past to the future through the present. Furthermore, there is no meaning or purpose for the present without the future. The present reality is structured in such a way that it contains its future, constituting an antecedent world for the world of tomorrow, the two worlds connected through such necessary scientific and philosophical principles as causation and continuity.

8. Time is the medium of evolutionary change of all things
The space-time continuum itself is evolving, as is everything in it. [138] All our experiences are within space-time. Things change in alignment with the forward-direction of time – nothing changes in a backwards direction.

9. Time is predominantly a carrier of high rates of change, motion (cosmological time) and pressures towards inherent entropic disorder (entropic time)
Futurology must take note of the behaviour of time and how it effects change in phenomena both in nature and society.

10. Psychological time is bi-directional
Psychological time gives access to past time through reconstruction of past events in human memory, whilst anticipating future time based on past experience. Recent neuropsychological evidence points to one neural network in the human brain which processes memories of the past and 'memories of the future'. This cognitive ability is viewed as an important evolutionary competitive advantage for humans. The past leaves traces both in the physical world, indicating past-evolution, and in the mind.

These ten propositions about time, derived from physics, cosmology, philosophy and neuropsychology, have theoretical implications. It is clear that orientation towards the future should be a fundamental human attitude, enjoying a cognitive priority over both past and present time. It is recommended that forecasts view the present and its conditions as transitional in the evolution of space-time towards the future.

Past-evolution gives important indicators of future-evolution depending on an entity's lifespan and lifecycles. Foresight needs to be balanced by hindsight, or knowledge of the past, as a form of 'collective memory', creating knowledge-based anticipation. Memory is where knowledge resides. Psychology has identified the inextricable link between retrospective and prospective memories. Futurists may use the reconstructed collective memory of past time to direct space-time trajectories open in present time to a lower-entropy future, in order to avoid high-entropy default future outcomes. This study will demonstrate that memories of the future are possible for sound neuropsychological and epistemological reasons.

Present time is the transition between collective memory of past time and the inherent direction towards the future. Being transitional by nature, the present is less important than both past time and future time. Present time locates entities on the timeline of their evolutionary lifespan, enabling predictions about their future evolution. Knowing the past-evolution of the subject being studied will help the futurist place its future-evolution more accurately.

The idea of the extended present, being several generations long, perhaps even as long as two hundred years, as postulated by Elise Boulding, [139] is consistent with the meaning of the space-time continuum and the continuity of time. This viewpoint also accommodates the crucial role of memory as a tool for ordering civilisation within entropic time. Not only is human existence inter-generational, with languages, norms, values and personality traits being passed down the 'time-chain' from generation to generation, but whole civilisations and cultures evolve over decades, centuries and even millennia. Time has huge evolutionary momentum.

In the 1918 introduction to *The Decline of the West*, German philosopher Oswald Spengler explained that both space and time have their own logic. The logic of space he identified as causation (a concept to be discussed in detail in the following chapter). He then described the 'organic necessity' of destiny as 'the logic of time'. [140] This necessity of time, he claimed, was the essence and kernel of all history. Between these two forces, the logic of space and the logic of time, the whole world is ordered. [141] Time, he claimed, has a destiny, a built-in rational purpose, working according to laws just as nature obeys laws like causation. The laws of history will be examined in Chapter 11. Time has deep meaning and is infused with purpose and impetus.

The understanding of time and the future illuminated by contemporary science has paved the way for a new science of foreknowledge. This was the dream of H.G. Wells. Enabling the creation of foreknowledge would fulfill a deep human desire and need. Over time this science would undeniably elevate civilisation to a more ordered level.

CHAPTER 9
GROUNDS FOR FOREKNOWLEDGE

Is knowledge of the future really attainable? To answer in the affirmative, we need a clear philosophical understanding of the world of the future. This chapter will outline five key principles responsible for shaping today's world into the world of tomorrow. These principles provide the theoretical grounds for foreknowledge. They will also be the philosophical foundation of an epistemology for futurology to be developed in Chapter 10.

While the study of the future aims at a 'systematic exploration of the future', [142] the general aim of philosophy, according to Bertrand Russell, is a theoretical understanding of the world. [143]

It is not uncommon for futurists to doubt the existence, or reality, of the future, so first, it is necessary to prove that the future is real, part of the continuity of time. We need to debunk the myth that the future is somehow disconnected from time.

In the space-time continuum, where space and time have been interconnected since the Big Bang, time is seen as an integral part of our experience of the external world. After Einstein there can be no separation or disconnection of time from space. That is why denying the reality of the future is like doubting the continuation of the space-time world itself beyond the present. Since space-time is billions of years old, it is absurd to think it will suddenly disappear.

Russell claims that the past and future must be acknowledged to be as real as the present because of the notion of continuity. [144] There is a continuity of space-time in which things evolve through past, present and future. There is no discernible boundary line between present and future. The evolutionary process of time is continuous. The world is a world-in-the-making. In *Adventures of Ideas,* the great philosopher Whitehead warned that the present would collapse if the future was cut away as it would be emptied of its content, meaning and purpose.

Spengler referred to the 'logic', or destiny, of time. Ever since time began, a continuous evolutionary process has been underway, moving into the future with predetermined purpose. From a cosmological, evolutionary perspective disconnecting the future from the whole of evolving reality would be short-sighted and even illogical. Yet this is exactly what is entailed by claiming that the future is unreal.

Just as time is immanent, or in-dwelling, in space, so the future is immanent in the process of time. The reality of the future is derived from time's basic spatial and evolutionary character. The future, wrote Whitehead, 'lives actively in its antecedent world…immanent in the present with some degree of structural definition'. [145]

The statement 'the future does not exist' is like saying 'nothing exists outside this moment', implying that we are trapped in an eternal present. That would be a position of extreme scepticism and solipsism. If applied consistently, such a position would probably undermine the whole of the scientific enterprise. (American logician Charles Sanders Peirce once said there are no such beings as 'absolute skeptics'. [146]) Fortunately, the future, as part of continuous time, is real.

The idea of a discontinuous future runs counter to the nature of reality and time. That is why it does not make sense to disconnect the future from our experience of time. On the basis of the union of time and space in one continuously evolving 4-D entity, it is perfectly reasonable to affirm the future's reality. Try telling a pregnant mother, or young graduate, or investor, or head of an R & D department that there's no future. Try to stop a seed from growing, or a flower from blooming in spring, or a mountain river from flowing into the valley below after the snows have melted. It is simply impossible to conceive of life without time or time without a future. The first principle in the case for the future is that the nature of space-time as an evolving continuum shows that the future is a continuous part of time's physical reality.

It is one thing to show that the future is real. It is quite another to prove it is knowable in terms of current scientific knowledge of the world. Knowledge of the world accumulated by science is based on the premise that there is sufficient regularity in nature to permit it to be modelled in theoretical terms. Recently, Hawking stated categorically: 'The universe is comprehensible because it is governed by scientific laws; that is to say, its behaviour can be modelled.' [147]

What this means is that the physical world is subject to proven laws: 'we appear to need only a handful of laws to explain pretty much all of physics….We currently have a theory that is demonstrably proven, after a vast and painstaking effort by thousands of scientists around the world, to work across a very wide range of phenomena'. [148] The lawfulness of nature, in other words, allows science to develop models explaining reality. More specifically, nature has been shown to operate through a few basic laws and forces: 'These four forces [gravity, electromagnetism, the strong nuclear force and the weak nuclear force] act between just twelve fundamental particles to build everything in the world we can see.' [149] There is a 'unified fabric of law' as well as 'richness of structure' in laws of nature. [150] Gravity, one of the four forces of nature, shapes not just galaxies, but also stars and planets, giving our universe its large-scale structure. At a smaller scale, the electromagnetic force structures atoms and molecules, while the strong nuclear force holds the atomic nuclei together. [151] Within this framework of deep structure, the universe teems with evolving matter, energy and, on earth, life-forms.

The master equation of physics, called the Standard Model of Particle Physics, testifies to the degree to which physics has mapped out the underlying laws governing nature. This master equation's function is 'to specify the rules according to which every particle in the entire universe interacts with every other particle (except it does not account for gravity)…Figuring out the master equation is without doubt one of the great achievements in the history of physics'. [152] The models physics has developed and proven to explain nature are the basis for making predictions about future behaviour conforming to scientific laws.

The second principle in the theory of how the world-in-the-making is formed from the world around us is that existence behaves lawfully over time, enabling scientific modelling and prediction of future states to take place. Chapter 11 looks at the laws of social evolution which enable us to watch the unfolding of the society of the future as today's society evolves into tomorrow's.

It must be acknowledged that the laws of nature, and social evolution, cannot always identify all the factors that might influence behaviour of an entity in the future: 'One must conceive of the laws of nature as necessary only if one abstracts from contingencies, representing essentially independent factors which may exist outside of the scope of things that can be treated by the laws under consideration.…Hence, we conceive of the necessity of a law of nature as conditional, since it applies only to the extent that these contingencies may be neglected. In many cases, they are, indeed, negligible.' [153]

As the last statement suggests, on balance, there are more causal influences decisively shaping tomorrow's world than there are contingencies which cause random behaviour. I cannot agree with American logician Peirce, for example, that irregularities in nature are much more frequent than regularities. [154] Only four major forces are responsible for keeping the whole universe together and physics has developed its master equation which explains *all* the relationships between all the components of nature, demonstrating a deep cohesion underlying its order. This means regularities are far more prevalent than irregularities at both the celestial and macroscopic levels of existence.

The reason why science does not claim that its laws and its knowledge of nature are absolute is due to the infinite and inexhaustible characteristics of nature which are in 'an infinite state of becoming'. [155] Bohm refers to the 'qualitative infinity of nature' [156] whereby complexity is brought about by constant motion with endless qualitative and quantitative change. Self-evidently, it is not possible to have complete, or absolute, knowledge of something that is infinite and ever-changing. [157] It is a long-held maxim of science that all models and theories are approximations of reality.

Behaviour in nature is neither entirely unpredictable nor entirely predictable. Unpredictability can arise from disturbances from outside any system in question: 'No mechanical system is ever completely isolated.... Disturbances arising outside the system will destroy the perfect one-to-one character of the connection.' [158] But the weight of evidence is currently with the causal rather than the contingent and totally unexpected. Nature as portrayed by contemporary physics is more like a kaleidoscope than a clock, with regularities working alongside chance events to produce endless arrangements of varying patterns. These patterns are knowable and discernible everywhere we look. Physicist and futurist Michio Kaku states that we can even apply these laws of nature to anticipate the future of technology itself.

The advancement of scientific knowledge of the universe has enabled humanity to deepen its understanding of how it works. [159] And this knowledge has reached a consensus that the universe is remarkably lawful in its behaviour: 'Many different lines of evidence show that the character of physical law has remained remarkably constant thus far in the history of the universe, and we have no indications that this trend will not continue....For example, studies of the early universe in the context of the big bang theory strongly suggest that the physical laws which describe nature are both fairly well understood and have held constant from very early times to the present.' [160] We can model and watch the world-in-the-making of the future because there is a deep structure of lawfulness evident in nature, symbolised by the Standard Model of Particle Physics.

Another aspect of the process of today's world transitioning into a different future world is the concept of antecedence: 'Everything is in a perpetual state of transformation, motion and change. However, we discover that nothing simply surges up out of nothing without having antecedents that existed before…everything comes from other things and gives rise to other things.' [161]

Antecedence, in short, conceives of the world as a deeply-interconnected reality which is in an infinite process of becoming whereby everything emerges and evolves from prior conditions, entities and systems, creating continuity between past, present and future evolutionary change. It shows that the behaviour of objects in nature is extensively influenced by various other bodies and forces around them.

One outcome of the endless process of antecedence is the influence of causation. Malthus, who predicted future problems for humanity as a result of exponential population growth, believed that the laws of nature and causation were the foundation of human knowledge. [162] Certainly, causation is a basis of much foreknowledge.

Einstein, in one of his few recorded statements about the future, described this phase of time as 'as necessary and determined as the past', given that there is a 'sense of universal causation' in nature. [163] In this statement, he proposes a deterministic concept of the future whereby the powerful effects of universal causation enable the scientist to study the future in the same way as the past.

Causality, the key concept in foreknowledge, is by no means excluded in relativity theory: 'cause and effect are sacred in Einstein's universe'.[164] Bertrand Russell defines a cause as 'an event or group of events of some known general character, and having a known relation to some other event, called the effect….What is actually known, as a matter of empirical science, is that certain constant relations are observed to hold between the members of a group of events at a certain time…any such constant relation between events of specified kinds with a given interval of time is a causal law….It states that there is a constant relation between causes of certain kinds and effects of certain kinds'. [165] Russell claimed that 'every event has a cause'. [166]

The concept of causality goes beyond association of factors and conditions: 'the future effects come out of past causes through a process satisfying necessary relationships...mere association is not enough to prove this kind of connection'. [167]

Physics has identified 'necessary relationships' between objects, events and conditions underlying the continuous processes of change in nature. These relationships are formulated into various laws, including causal laws: 'The general category of law, which includes the causal laws, the laws of chance, and the laws relating these two classes of law, we shall call by the name of the laws of nature.' [168]

A strong connectivity between cause and effect is what distinguishes a true cause from a random association. 'An important way of obtaining evidence in favor of the assumption that a given set of events or conditions comes necessarily from another, is to show that a wide range of changes in one or more of the presumed causes occurring under conditions in which other factors are held constant always produces corresponding changes in the effects. The more coordinates of this kind that one can demonstrate in the changes of the two sets of events, the stronger is the evidence that they are causally related.' [169]

Bohm distinguishes between background causes, which he calls conditions, and immediate causes: 'The conditions may be defined as those factors which are necessary for the production of the results in question, but which do not change sufficiently in the context of interest to produce an appreciable change in the effects.' [170]

Background conditions, which have causal impacts, are a key area of study in futurology: 'basic qualities and properties of each kind of entity depend not only on their substructures but also on what is happening in their general background'. [171]

Knowledge of causation enables scientific observers to make predictions: 'the new properties are predicted on the basis of the notion implicit in the concept of causality, that changes that have been found to take place in the past will occur again in the future if similar conditions are reproduced.' [172] Bell explains: 'Whenever some empirical correlation exists between two variables, it is possible to use one to predict the other....The prediction will be accurate only so long as the relationship continues.' [173]

There are several categories of causal relationships. Firstly, there is a one-to-many relationship (i.e. one cause to many effects). Secondly, there are many-to-one relationships (i.e. many causes for same effect) 'where many different kinds of causes can produce essentially the same effect'.[114] Thirdly, the holy grail of scientific enquiry is the one-to-one relationship between one cause and one effect: 'Within the general framework of one-to-many and many-to-one causal relationships, the one-to-one relationship is then an idealization which is never realized perfectly.'[115]

Causation and the conformity of behaviour to observable laws is the basis of predictive knowledge: 'From past observation…we may conclude that x causes y….Knowledge, or partial knowledge, of the past, often expressed in theoretical or quasi-theoretical statements about relationships, can be applied inferentially to the future, although, obviously, not with certainty.'[116] Causes, by definition, always produce effects subsequent in time, located in the future relative to the cause.[117]

The interplay between causality and chance determines what is knowable and predictable in nature. The relationship between the operations of causes and the events of chance are complementary, like two sides of a coin. Both the causal description of an event, or object, and the contingent description are 'partial views' only: 'Each view… limits the other, corrects the other, and through its relationship with the other, enables us to form a better concept of what the object is.'[118] Due to the infinite scale and complexity of nature it is not possible to trace all influences directly to identifiable causes; however, there are both immediate causes and background conditions which influence a great deal of future behaviour.[119]

We have seen how the world-in-the-making of the future emerges from antecedent conditions. The final jigsaw piece in this picture of how the world of today gives way to patterns which will define its future state is the concept of lifecycles. In particular, they enable future-watching to determine time scales of future evolution.

The evolutionary function of time, and the location of all change within the continuous process of time, results in the ubiquity of lifecycles. Lifecycles can be seen as: 'The complete series of stages through which an organism passes…to its eventual death.'[120] An organism or entity passes through changes of state as it grows, evolves and eventually expires. Lifecycles occur from cosmological to atomic levels of existence. Time is the medium in which they are worked out.

In cosmology, the universe itself has a lifespan. It has a definite age.[181] So do the objects and phenomena in it: 'Our biography of the universe, and the study of astrophysics in general, plays out in four important size scales: planets, stars, galaxies, and the universe as a whole....On each of these size scales, astrophysical objects go through lifecycles....On the largest size scale, we can view the universe as a single evolving entity and study its life cycle....Current astronomical data strongly suggest that the fate of our universe lies in continued expansion.' [182]

Galaxies, solar systems, stars and planets all have lifecycles; that is, these entities have definite beginnings, phases of growth and decline and expected expiry dates. It is thought galaxies will 'evaporate their stars out into intergalactic space after only about twenty cosmological decades.' [183] Stars have a lifespan, [184] as do black holes. [185] Planets will eventually all turn into radiation at the end of their existence cycle. [186] 'The sun, centre of our solar system and provider of life-giving heat and energy on earth, is about half-way through its expected twelve-billon-year lifespan [187] – and it will eventually expire as its hydrogen supply runs low. Earth itself has a lifespan, with an expected two billion years left before the sun incinerates it. [188]

In biology, organisms have lifecycles. A species 'starts with just a few members, reaches a maximum population at some point, and then typically declines to just a few individuals before going extinct.'[189] It is estimated that of the millions of species which have existed on earth, ninety-seven percent have become extinct. [190]

Even at the sub-atomic level, the particle known as the proton has a lifespan, albeit a very long one: 'Long thought to be stable and infinitely long-lived, protons can decay into smaller particles if given enough time... the time required for proton decay is about 30 cosmological decades (10^{30} years).' [191]

The whole of the natural order lives out its existence in evolving space-time, with all entities having cycles within predetermined lifespans. It is this tapestry of recurring lifecycles and universal patterns in nature which allows the natural sciences to make predictions about future evolutionary paths of entities.

Lifecycles, the patterns formed within life spans are, then, ubiquitous. What is of interest to the futurologist is how they form patterns which can be identified, studied and analysed. It is their patterns and trajectories, whether bell-shaped or S-shaped, which may be used by futurists as a tool for building up knowledge-pictures of the future. Patterns over time are like knowledge-pictures which help the futurist to foresee the future. Many phenomena comply with a sigmoid (S) growth curve, showing exponential growth in early stages followed by a levelling-off after 'natural control factors such as space, the availability of food and the accumulation of waste in the local environment' [192] slow down and restrict the growth pattern. Readers will be familiar with the typical S-curve life cycle in technology, an important element of social change, passing through conception, development, expansion, maturity and obsolescence. The bell-shaped lifespans of finite resources like fossil fuels enabled Hubbert to make accurate forecasts of production peaks for both the US and the world (see Figure 8).

If one plotted the whole life history of an entity in 4-D space-time, it would yield its world line. This is a complete set of all the positions the object has had in the world, with each position having a time label to indicate when the object was there. Needless to say, world lines would be very long, time-consuming to construct and not especially useful. So we will stick to the large-scale patterns of development called lifecycles in both the natural and social worlds.

Chapter 11 will reveal the existence of cycles of socio-economic development manifested through history. Historians led by Arnold Toynbee have studied around twenty-five civilisations which had a duration of over 500 years (and about fifty civilisations and empires lasting 200 years or less). Complexity scientist and futurological theoretician Robert Samet traces the dramatic decline in the average duration of empires over history: 'The earliest civilisations between 3500 BC and AD 500 lasted for an average of over 2,000 years....In the period AD 500–1500, the average duration of an empire was 500–1,000 years....Since AD 1500...the average duration has been 200–500 years.' [193] This means the lifespan of socio-political empires averaged 2,000 years for a period of four millennia, but then more than halved within the next 1,000 years of history. This sharp decrease in the lifespan of civilisations accelerated yet again in the following 500 years of history, dropping to a little over one-tenth of their average duration in ancient times. This is the deep trend of history. It would be foolish to believe this can be easily reversed. These results show that civilisations have lifecycles, too, and their durations are shrinking over time.

Samet gives the average time taken for a society to progress from a traditional pastoral community to a complex post-industrial information society as 240 years. [194] Evolutionary processes in nature and society tend to follow such regular time-spans. Kondratieff identified long economic waves of roughly sixty years (see Chapter 11).

Samet explains how shorter business cycles operate within the long economic waves: 'In essence, infrastructure investment and city building cycles result in construction cycles of some twenty to twenty-five years… that are synchronized within the long wave data, and this forms the background to the phenomenon of property cycles.' [195] From the cosmos to civilisation, from stars to societies, from galaxies to gadgets, everything has a lifespan, and within its duration of existence, a lifecycle shape, or time pattern.

The fifth principle in the philosophical case for knowing the future is that the ubiquity of lifecycles, or patterns of development within a lifespan, in nature and society, means phenomena may be located on a timeline showing past-evolution, present state and anticipated future-evolution.

In a similar vein, Samet argues that the main features of his evolutionary approach to the future deal with path dependence (a concept in complexity science like Bohm's idea of antecedence in physics), emergence, macrolaws, civil or societal transitions, macrosystem design and the absorption of extreme events. [196] Patterns of society's evolutionary past 'foretell' the shape of its future.

In conclusion, the five theoretical principles providing grounds for foreknowledge may be schematically represented.

The principle of antecedence provides the context for the continuous emergence of new objects, phenomena and behaviour from pre-existing ones in a deeply inter-connected, ever-changing world. In a quasi-deterministic view of time, the future is not materially and substantially different from the past. Rather it is evolving slowly in an extended present according to the laws of nature and social order. Patterns of the past get repeated in the future.

The five philosophical principles of foreknowledge shown in Figure 9 challenge the assumption that the future is eternally elusive, doomed to be a domain of uncertainty. It is this idea which has long presented a

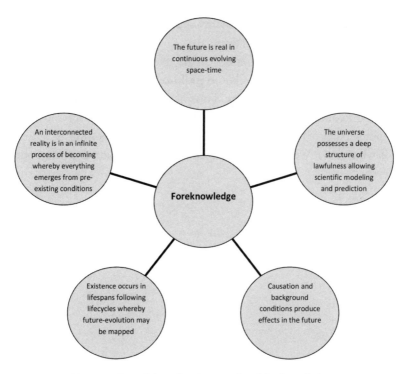

Figure 9. Five philosophical principles of foreknowledge

theoretical stumbling block to the establishment of futurology as a science.

Although Figure 9 shows the strong grounds for knowing the future, the underlying worldview of quasi-determinism does not signify that the future is mechanically pre-determined as it was in Newton's model of the world. As futurist Wendell Bell explains: 'To say that something is determined is not necessarily to say that it is inevitable. It is simply to say that some causes and effects can be identified with some degree of probable connection under specified conditions.' [197]

Einstein stated that universal causation in nature applies as equally to the future as it does to the past. The doctrine of quasi-determinism is consistent with the principle of antecedence in physics whereby all things emerge from other things through an infinite process of becoming. It is also consistent with the space-time continuum and the continuity of time.

This is the case for foreknowledge. In this view, the future of the world can be mapped out and pictured. It seems counter-intuitive to say this, but only because we have believed myths about the future for so long. We have not understood the nature of time.

When the combined effect of the five principles in Figure 9 is considered, there seems to be no philosophical reason why humans cannot acquire foreknowledge. Futurology has a deep-seated logic to it. Consequently, an opportunity has opened up to develop a proper epistemology of futurology. The 'impossible' dream of knowing the future, in which H.G. Wells believed, is beginning to turn into a reality before our eyes.

CHAPTER 10
AN EPISTEMOLOGY FOR FUTUROLOGY

The scientific and human importance of the future is beyond question. Now we need methods by which we can gain knowledge of it.

The word epistemology is derived from the Greek word *episteme*, [198] meaning knowledge. It is defined as 'concerned with the nature, sources and limits of knowledge' [199] and as a 'theory of knowledge…with regard to its methods, validity, and scope'. [200] Knowledge, in turn, is seen as 'certain understanding, as opposed to opinion'. [201] Broadly, any belief that a proposition is true, that it constitutes knowledge, needs to be grounded in observation and reasons. [202]

American logician and philosopher Charles Sanders Peirce described the objective of reasoning as finding out from what we already know *something else which we do not know.* [203] The scientific method itself is based on progressing from known and observed facts, to what Peirce called the Unknown. The future, to this point, has been part of this Unknown, beyond the current frontier of knowledge.

Logic has principles for ensuring the validity of the thought processes and methods by which previously unknown material is derived from existing knowledge. In his treatise on probability, which Alfred North Whitehead regarded as a classic text on the subject, John Maynard Keynes spoke about a body of direct knowledge which allows propositions regarding 'indirect knowledge' to be made after following valid arguments: 'We claim rational grounds for assertions which are not conclusively demonstrated. We allow…that statements may be (as yet) unproved, without, for that reason, being unfounded.' [204] In Keynes' model, a set of propositions compiles evidence from direct knowledge to build well-founded, as-yet-unproven, propositions which yield new, indirect knowledge.

The prerequisite of all knowledge of the future is that it should be gained from current knowledge using valid logic. In this process, the futurologist should articulate the rational connection, or argument, which bridges current knowledge and foreknowledge.

The most common way to do this is through the method of induction by which a new fact is inferred from the properties of facts stated in the premises of the argument. The flow of this familiar logical process is visible in Figure 10.

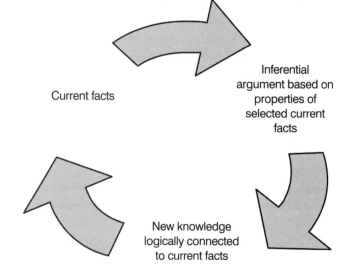

Current facts

Inferential argument based on properties of selected current facts

New knowledge logically connected to current facts

Figure 10. Purpose and method of induction

A futurological epistemology may be based on this established method of gaining new knowledge: 'It has been widely thought that all knowledge of matters of fact that we have observed must be based on inductive inferences from what we have observed. In particular, all knowledge of the future is, on this view, based on induction.' [205]

Inferences typically generalise from observations of behaviour of particular objects to the whole set of these objects. [206] The generalisation assumes, on clear and reasonable grounds, that some pattern has been detected which is universal to the whole set of the object(s) under scrutiny and can therefore be applied to every similar occurrence of the phenomenon in the future.

Inductive inferences take a set of observed occurrences of a phenomenon, which we can call for convenience fact A, as providing logical grounds for stating a principle, law or conclusion which extends the knowledge of fact A to fact A+.

A simple example will illustrate this process of inference. Take a bag containing a large unknown mixture of, say, black and white marbles. Then use a sample to determine the approximate ratio of black to white marbles in the bag. This will give fact A, namely, the ratio of the random sample (say two black marbles for every white one). The given fact A is then inferred to reflect the total distribution of black and white marbles in the bag, which becomes the inferred fact A+. It is easier to count the sample than all the marbles. In logic and life, inference is an exceptionally useful tool.

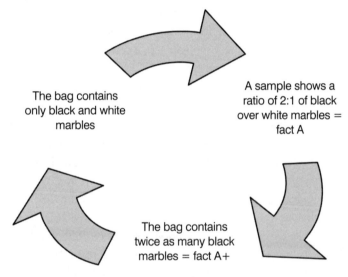

The bag contains only black and white marbles

A sample shows a ratio of 2:1 of black over white marbles = fact A

The bag contains twice as many black marbles = fact A+

Figure 11. Inferring fact A+ from sample fact A

In Figure 11, an additional, previously unknown, piece of information is gained from current knowledge, and available evidence, through a process of inference. If the marbles have been properly and evenly mixed, one may assume that the sample ratio of black to white ones observed in the random count will be representative of the whole bag. If the random sample which gave us fact A is large enough to be considered representative, it is highly likely that fact A+ will be at least a very good approximation. This inferential method used to extend knowledge is logical and reasonable.

Another example of inductive acquisition of new knowledge is the calculation of the total energy emitted by the sun by Sir John Herschel in 1838 after conducting an experiment using a can of water, a thermometer and an umbrella. In cloudless, sunny conditions, Herschel covered the can with an umbrella and let the water in the tin heat up from ambient warmth. With the sun directly overhead, he took the temperature. Then he removed the shade. As expected, direct sunlight heated up the water much more rapidly. Taking a second reading, he was able to work out the exact amount of energy delivered to the can by direct sunlight. He extrapolated this energy output to a square metre, and then to the entire surface of earth. After factoring in the average orbital distance to the sun, namely 150 million kilometres, Herschel estimated the total energy that the sun gives off. His calculation employed a considerable inductive leap from one simple, and useless, fact – how much energy had been delivered to the can of water by direct sunlight – to a generalised, useful piece of scientific knowledge about our sun.

The principle of induction, argues epistemological scholar, Laurence BonJour, is based on the idea that 'unobserved and merely possible instances are likely to resemble observed instances'. [207] The method for acquiring prognostic knowledge must follow exactly the same inductive process. Induction, the use of inferences, is one of humanity's greatest cognitive tools. Audi states that there is no limit in epistemology to the richness of ideas and theories which can be produced by this method. [208]

It is obvious from the start that inferences depend for their success on the regularities that are found in nature and in society. Otherwise it would not be logical to generalise from an observation of a sample, fact A, to a wider set, producing fact A+. The deep structure of lawfulness elucidated in the previous chapter implies that there is fertile ground for the inductive method to accumulate knowledge on a virtually unlimited basis.

What is important about such inferred knowledge is that it should be justified, based on solid, 'undefeated' evidence. While logic investigates the principles of valid thought, [209] epistemology determines the grounds of true knowledge. Only justified knowledge of the future is going to be acceptable and useful: 'The term "justification" belongs to a cluster of normative terms that also includes "rational", "reasonable" and "warranted"…epistemologists are concerned with what it takes for a belief to be justified, rational, reasonable or warranted.' [210] Audi states that knowledge can be increased in two ways, namely, by gaining new content (e.g. a new fact), a process which he calls inferential extension, or by reinforcing the grounds for believing what we already know through

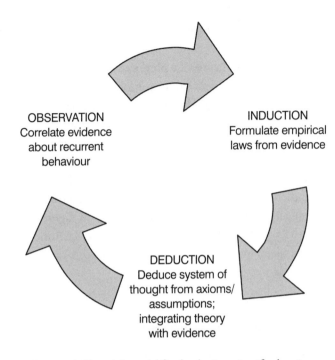

OBSERVATION
Correlate evidence
about recurrent
behaviour

INDUCTION
Formulate empirical
laws from evidence

DEDUCTION
Deduce system of
thought from axioms/
assumptions;
integrating theory
with evidence

Figure 12. Einstein's model for developing scientific theories

inferential strengthening. Both kinds of knowledge are based on inductive inferences. [211]

The vital role of induction in scientific theory-building has been well described by Einstein: 'From a systematic theoretical point of view, we may imagine the process of evolution of an empirical science to be a continuous process of induction. Theories are evolved and are expressed… as statements of a large number of individual observations in the form of empirical laws, from which the general laws can be ascertained by comparison…but this point of view by no means embraces the whole of the actual process; for it slurs over the important part played by intuition and deductive thought in the development of an exact science. As soon as a science has emerged from its initial stages, theoretical advances are no longer achieved merely by a process of arrangement. Guided by empirical data, the investigator, rather, develops a system of thought, which, in general, is built up logically from a small number of fundamental assumptions, the so-called axioms. We call such a system of thought a theory. The theory finds justification for its existence in the fact that it correlates a large number of single observations, and it is just here that the "truth" of the theory lies.' [212]

Einstein argues that theories are produced after an inductive process consisting of a number of observations consolidated into empirical laws, which, in turn, are then arranged by the scientific 'investigator' into a larger system of thought, or theory. [213] The process of induction sorts a series of observations into laws following which deductive thinking connects these laws into a wider theory, or model. Fact and theory are always intertwined. In *Adventures of Ideas* Whitehead wrote that while theories are built upon facts, facts themselves are infused with theoretical interpretation. The interrelationship between fact and theory is clear in Figure 12, which illustrates the key steps of the process for forming scientific theories. Hawking stipulates four criteria of a good scientific theory: 'A model is a good model if it:

1. Is elegant

2. Contains few arbitrary or adjustable elements

3. Agrees with and explains all existing observations

4. Makes detailed predictions about future observations that can disprove or falsify the model if they are not borne out.' [214]

The final arbiter for scientific truth remains experiment, that is, observed, evidence. [215] A scientific theory begins and ends with observational evidence, as suggested by the virtuous cycle in Figure 12 which continuously refers back to the step of observation. [216] Whitehead stated that all knowledge is derived from, and verified by, direct observation. In epistemology, this kind of empirical knowledge is called *a posteriori*, that is, coming after experience, not before.

It is a precondition of all knowledge that it should be validated and justified. Williams (2001) defines knowledge as justified true belief. [217] I would like to focus for a minute on the criterion of reasonableness as a useful concept for understanding validated knowledge of the future. Reasonable means: based on reason, derived from sound judgement, implying a fair consideration of all available evidence. Valid propositions are ones which have not been overturned by counter-arguments or contrary evidence.

Jurisprudence developed the important principle of 'proof beyond a reasonable doubt'. This is the standard of evidence required for a fair criminal conviction in most legal systems, including in the US and UK. This does not necessarily require absolute certainty. But it does require, as in logic, a strong rational connection between the conclusion reached and the totality of the evidence available.

BonJour has indicated that most recent philosophers have argued that knowledge does not require conclusive proof but only 'reasonably strong reasons…to make it quite likely that the proposition in question is true, but not necessarily strong enough to guarantee its truth…presumably more than fifty-one percent probability is required'. [218] The truth of futurological statements will rest on the amount of evidence upon which they are based.

As the First World War was commencing, Bertrand Russell established the epistemological grounds for a futurology. In a series of lectures in 1914, in which he argued that philosophy needed to become scientific in order to produce more effective results, this major modern philosopher opined that scientific knowledge of the future was, indeed, possible: 'Knowledge concerning the future – which is the kind of knowledge that must be sought if we are to know about human destiny – is possible within certain narrow limits. It is impossible to say how much the limits may be enlarged with the progress of science. But what is evident is that any proposition about the future belongs by its subject-matter to some particular science, and is to be ascertained, if at all, by the methods of that science.' [219]

Russell claimed it was theoretically possible to gain empirical knowledge of the future as part of a special social science. Today, this science is generally called Futures Studies. However, as explained earlier, this field of enquiry has come to see itself as more of an art than a science. Once an epistemology of the future has been developed, this term could be replaced with a more formal, precise word like Futurology.

Russell asked his audience in these 1914 lectures 'What is the principle of inference by which we pass from past sunrises to future ones?' He then laid down a stringent standard for such inferred knowledge of the future: 'If inferences as to the future are valid, what principle must be involved in making them? The principle involved is the principle of induction, which, if it is true, must be an *a priori* logical law, not capable of being proved or disproved.' [220]

With this last statement, we have reached a crucial stage in the search for the basis of foreknowledge, a point of no return. In fact, this 1914 lecture is a milestone in the search for a science of the future. It is vital to understand what Russell means here because he is setting out a logical standard for valid futuristic inferences. The epistemic bridge between the known and unknown is one of the most important of all cognitive tools. The logic should be based on valid and universal principles, such as the laws of causation and evidence of evolutionary lifecycles discussed in the previous chapter.

Russell reasoned that future-based inferences are only valid if they are backed up by some *a priori* truth or principle. *A priori* in epistemology refers to a kind of knowledge that does not require empirical or sensory evidence to be proved. Examples of *a priori* truths are axioms of mathematics or the famous 'I think, therefore I am' of Descartes. This self-evident statement is true not because of any evidence but simply because its contradiction would itself be a self-contradiction.

Deductive reasoning often involves *a priori* statements of truth, such as in the well-known syllogism: All men are mortal; Socrates is mortal; therefore Socrates is mortal. There is no need to seek evidence to prove this conclusion: it follows automatically from combining the truth of its two premises.

In inductive reasoning, by contrast, *a priori* justification 'involves a direct insight…into the nature and structure of reality…reflecting features and relations that could not fail to obtain'. [221] This is a critical point. Such *a priori* knowledge results from 'directly apprehending necessary relations between the universals with which we are acquainted'. [222] To satisfy Russell's epistemological standard, we will need some *a priori* empirical principle which links knowledge of the structure of current reality and knowledge of the future with a strong logical bridge.

By contrast, the logic of *a priori* deductive truths inheres in the sequence of ideas itself, based on the force of reason alone. These truths draw only on the meaning of concepts themselves, to form certain conclusions (as in the above syllogism). *A priori* justification in induction, however, does not depend on this kind of rational power of ideas. Instead, it refers to a proven, built-in feature of reality known by empirical science.

How can futurology rise to Russell's logical challenge of finding an *a priori* inductive justification for its inferences? The answer lies in a principle discussed in the previous chapter as providing reasonable philosophical grounds for building up knowledge of the future: causation. Causation is, indeed, an *a priori* law of empirical science. It is a phenomenon built into the structure of reality as revealed by centuries of evidence. Russell defines it as 'a general proposition in virtue of which it is possible to infer the existence of one thing or event from the existence of another or a number of others.' [223]

The *a priori* character of causation he explained as follows: 'The law of causation, according to which later events can theoretically be predicted by means of earlier events, has often been held to be *a priori*, a necessity of thought, a category without which science would be impossible.' [224]

This study adopts an empirical and logical approach to knowledge of the future and embraces causation as the ground of futurological inferences.

It was perhaps the universality of causation in a scientific worldview, whereby future events 'are just as determined as the past', which led Russell to make a mysterious statement about the future: 'It is a mere accident that we have no memory of the future.' [225] In this statement, he implies that it is theoretically possible to have memory of the future. Will scientific foresight produced by futurologists become detailed and accurate enough to create these hypothetical memories of the future through future knowledge?

For Russell, causation implies 'a relation of succession or co-existence between the thing given and the thing inferred'. [226] He insisted that inferences about the future need to state 'how much later' the effect is likely to happen, providing a more or less exact temporal value to the future inference.

In practice, futurists can draw up a causal map to apply the principle of causation in their work. Mind-maps can be very useful for structuring thoughts and visualising complex relationships between variables. In the same way, we can think of using causal maps to guide the futurist to the most probable future. Suppose we wanted to forecast the future of the global economy to, say, 2030. What influences, both direct and environmental, will determine the future shape of the global economy by 2030.

Figure 13 (page 82) is not an exhaustive causal map. Nevertheless, it does highlight key areas of causation in determining its most likely outcome. Even though there are several other causal factors which will affect this future state, such as the activities of the global capital markets, already a complex web of mutual influences has emerged. The causal map shows the factors which bring about change.

The futurist would determine the relative influences of factors like these, with some causal relations considered as primary, others as secondary and still others as having a more peripheral, indirect influence on the future outcome.

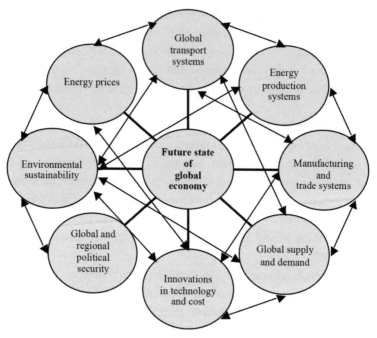

Figure 13. Simplified causal map for the future of the global economy

With causation, the observation of uniformities leads to a perfectly rational expectation of their future recurrence. Science goes further and has developed a principle which states that as the number of instances of such associations and regularities increases, the probability-relation between the given fact and the inferred fact 'approaches indefinitely near to certainty'. [227]

This is a startling principle, of great relevance to futurology and to humanity. It raises the possibility of certain knowledge of the future. The word 'certainty' is used here in the context of inferences about the future. The greater the coherence and frequency of the associations demonstrated by futurists in their forecasts and foresight, the more likely they are to produce highly credible, and, in some cases, *certain* knowledge. This principle holds virtually unlimited promise in terms of understanding our evolving destiny and preparing for our future. We could produce future knowledge with an accuracy the ancients and early moderns could not even have dreamt about. We would finally be armed with vivid memories of the future.

Russell's inductive principle, then, states categorically that some causal logic is required for valid inferences to the future: 'Whether inferences from past to future are valid depends wholly…upon the inductive principle: if it is true, such inferences are valid; if it is false, they are invalid.'[228]

This principle, 'using causal laws to support inferences from the observed to the unobserved',[229] is the logical foundation for futurology.

Following BonJour, I identify three approaches to the question of what constitutes the truth of knowledge, each of which has a bearing on how we will justify futurological assertions going forward. Firstly, foresight should be derived from established empirical truths about current reality and its universally observed structures. It should possess a strong initial correspondence to reality. Secondly it must also be logically self-consistent (coherent), satisfying logical principles. Third, foresight should lead to a high success rate in practice by producing accurate and useful prognostic knowledge, or Russell's 'memories of the future'. Was not Condorcet's anticipatory vision of equal political rights for women a far-sighted 'memory of the future'? Futurological work should set itself high epistemological standards in the process of establishing itself as a science. For that reason, it should satisfy all three criteria.

Futurology should, in my view, hold itself accountable to a narrow band of truth ranging from certain knowledge, based on direct causational influences, to highly probable knowledge, tracing influences of background conditions on future events and future evolution. Prognostications should exclude forecasts which are barely probable. They would not meet the epistemological standards required for a genuine social science.

As in Figure 14 (page 84), probability is usually measured on a scale of 0 to 1, with 0 denoting impossibility and 1 indicating certainty or something which is bound to happen.[230]

Figure 8. Narrow band of truth (◀—) for futurology on probability scale

To find out how futurological knowledge can meet the standard represented in Figure 14, restricting itself to prognostications which are either certain or highly probable, [231] it is necessary to understand key principles of the theory of probability.

Keynes defines 'probable' as 'a lower degree of rational belief than certainty'. [232] Note in this definition that probability is a form of rational belief even though it falls short of certainty. This suggests an element of objective probability, with a clear logic underpinning this form of indirect knowledge, establishing a strong correlation between the material that is known and the material that is not-yet-known.

Probable knowledge is gained through the standard method of inference: 'The theory of probability deals with the relation between two sets of propositions, such that, if the first set is known to be true, the second can be known with the approximate degree of probability by argument from the first.' [233] Probability is based on the fact that belief, or well-founded knowledge, is, in Keynes' words, 'capable of degree'. [234] This is a very important point to grasp. There are degrees of knowledge and rational belief ranging from certain to probable. Keynes characterises certainty itself as maximum probability.

The idea of probability is often illustrated by the example of throwing a die. Dice have six faces and each one has an equal probability of landing facing upwards. So the probability of rolling a 4 is ⅙ and the probability of rolling a 2 or 3 is ⅓. Although we will not expect to measure probable futurological knowledge with this kind of exactness, it will be possible to apply a probability weighting.

Ordinarily on this 0–1 scale, 0.51 would be the minimum level of probability required for knowledge, since it is not reasonable to say that a belief is probable if there are equally weighty reasons for saying it is improbable. However, the narrow band of truth in Figure 14 would regard a 0.66 degree of probability as a minimum standard given that there should be significantly greater likelihood of a prognostication occurring than not occurring. A prognostication with a high probability will have a correspondingly low probability of error. The reasons for the likelihood of it actually occurring as forecast would be much more convincing and weighty than any contrary evidence suggesting it would not happen. The likely outcome would be proven beyond a reasonable doubt after weighing up evidence for and against the probability of it happening. There would be persuasive empirical grounds for justifying the proposition.

Whitehead wrote that probability is always relative to evidence. A prognostication of high probability will be supported by overwhelming evidence in its favour. Audi states that a probability of just over 0.50, with little more than a fifty-fifty chance of being true, would not indicate good reasoning. It would mean the conclusion reached has about the same chance of being true as it has of being false. There would be too much doubt and uncertainty. By contrast, knowledge has to be so well-grounded that there is little room for doubt. It has to be shown to be objectively true beyond reasonable doubt. This should be true for foreknowledge, too.

The theory of probability is significant for predictive knowledge in general and for foresight production in particular. How should futurists take account of comparatively random and unpredictable events, ranging from high-impact Black Swan historical events to minor unforeseen changes?

In principle, predictive knowledge is possible for even apparently random events of this nature: 'By randomness we mean just that this independence leads to fluctuation of these contingencies in a very complicated way over a wide range of possibilities, but in such a manner that statistical averages have a regular and approximately predictable behaviour...one of the most characteristic features of chance fluctuations is that in a long enough time or in a large enough aggregate, every possible combination of events or objects will eventually occur.' [235]

Statistical aggregates, or averages over time, enable statistical laws to be formulated, rendering so-called chance fluctuations understandable and susceptible to analysis and prediction: 'in the long-run, and on the average, the relative frequency with which a given result will be obtained will fluctuate near a value that tends to come closer and closer to its probability'. [236]

The word 'probable' is derived from the Latin *probare* meaning to test or demonstrate, indicating that the veracity of a proposition about a probable occurrence may be tested or proven through reasons and/

or evidence. The word does imply some element of uncertainty in the proposition, the possibility of a chance variation occurring. While there are always good grounds for an assertion regarding any probable occurrence, caution is still required regarding the possible influence of chance variables. Hacking wrote that probability makes us think of the degree of confidence we can have in something uncertain in view of what we are able to find out about it. [237]

Even chance events and influences have deeper underlying causes. The scientist looks for these deeper relationships which are not apparent when looking at a random event in isolation or on the surface. There are different kinds of regularities behind the irregular behaviour observed in random events. In particular, established forecasting practice distinguishes between trends, seasonal patterns, cyclical patterns and random fluctuations which cannot fit into these regular relationships [238] between variables.

In determining probabilities, Keynes uses the criterion of evidential weight derived by balancing favourable and unfavourable evidence regarding the statement of probability. Here we can return to the jurisprudential concept of 'beyond a reasonable doubt' to support his theory of weighting: 'The weight…measures the sum of the favourable and unfavourable evidence, the probability measures the difference.' [239]

As evidence in favour of the probability-relation increases, the field of possibility is narrowed to a smaller universe of alternatives and propositions about a probable future reality. The relative frequency with which any associations forming the basis of a futurological inference occur will be important evidence for the probability weighting. This is because a frequency relation will be based on the way reality has been observed to work.

It would be difficult to overestimate the role evidence, and weighting, plays in logical probability. Relative to all the available evidence examined, it has to be reasonable to hold a 'high degree of belief' [240] in any statement of probability.

One variation of probability which is useful in futurology is conditional probability, typically phrased in the form 'if B happens, then it is highly probable that A will happen'. This type of probability statement contrasts with the categorical kind when there is no such condition, but rather some sort of direct cause or invariable relation.

So far, we have looked at futurological statements conveying certain or highly probable knowledge. We have also mentioned conditionally probable knowledge. All of these kinds of futurological knowledge have to be based on existing direct knowledge, whether facts or principles.

In conclusion, futurists may aim to make inductive inferences about future realities which are certain, highly probable or conditionally probable, adhering to the principles of logic. Futurology is philosophically consistent with what physics teaches about space-time, the arrow of time and the invisible structures and laws of reality. In seeking grounds for making logical and empirical statements about the future of the world, there should be a clear chain of logic connecting direct knowledge of the world with indirect knowledge of the future. To secure this chain of logic from present reality to future reality, it is necessary to use the *a priori* inductive principle described in 1914 by Bertrand Russell, which we concluded would have to be the doctrine of universal causation. This alone can be the basis of any certain knowledge of the future.

For statements in general to be verifiable, Russell contended, they should be such that any observer can discover them to be true. The ultimate test for a proposition about the future will be the retrospective evaluation after the time span specified in the forecast has passed. Before that point is reached, futurological knowledge should pass the epistemological tests outlined in this chapter. We are looking for highly probable or certain foreknowledge rather than any absolute certainty, an ideal which epistemologist Audi argues is unattainable. Absolute certainty is neither adequate for a real theory of knowledge nor appropriate for the human condition itself. That is not what science is aiming for.

In sum, sound and realistic philosophical and epistemological principles have been established for a discipline of Futurology.

But there is one more critical mystery to solve before we embark on our journey into the future of the world. Without this key, we will never break through the knowledge barrier that keeps what we know about the world locked inside the present time. We will remain blind to humanity's destiny. We are looking for the key of history. This will reveal the principles of social development to enable logical inferences about the future world to be made.

Can the riddle of whether societies operate according to laws of evolution be solved? Are there principles of social evolution which are as accessible to scientific investigation as those which govern nature? If society evolves according to laws which have been evident throughout history, then there would be nothing stopping futurists from applying the epistemological principles outlined in this chapter to generate accurate knowledge of the social future. If there are no such laws, however, the search for a new social science of the future would, in all likelihood, be doomed.

CHAPTER 11
THE KEY OF HISTORY

Everything is changing all of the time. Since the beginning of space-time, the universe, and everything in it, has been evolving. In general, entities change through a succession of states during their life careers. This succession takes place through continuous time, which is a medium in which all lifecycles take their course and their direction. The most common states things pass through are birth, growth, decline and death, providing a fundamental pattern or template of change. Although time in physics is a conveyor belt of high rates of change and even disorder, these underlying lifecycle patterns provide a basis for social prognosis. Future states can be plotted on an anticipated lifespan.

In Chapter 9, it was suggested that lifecycles are ubiquitous, from the cosmology of the universe to the lifespan of technologies. There are lifecycles and patterns of change in the evolution of society. So, have sociologists and historians found evidence of recurrent cycles of social change? Do socio-cultural entities, from households to organisations, from cultures to the great civilisations themselves, evolve according to universal patterns? Are there established laws of social evolution which form a body of socio-historical knowledge from which inferences about the social future can legitimately, or logically, be made?

The importance of these questions resides in the fact that it is the degree to which behaviour is lawful, conforming to scientific laws and principles, which determines whether or not a recurrence of such behaviour in future may be predicted. Historian Ian Morris makes a similar point when he says that the laws of history 'give us a pretty good sense of what is likely to happen next'. [241] But what exactly are these laws of history he has detected? Is there a key to history?

Forecasts of the social and economic future by the early prognostic thinkers, from Condorcet to H.G. Wells, from Jevons to M. King Hubbert, yielded significant and accurate insights, based on theories identifying key drivers of long-term development in society. Yet none of their theories could be considered complete, or mature, from a futurological perspective. In order to strengthen the theoretical basis of long-term social foresight, it is necessary to investigate more fully the scientific basis for studying the social future.

Systems thinking offers an illuminating view of the world with principles which apply equally to natural and social systems. In particular, the branch of systems thinking called Biomatrix theory provides a framework for explaining interconnections between nature and society within one huge web of life. Biomatrix theory shows that social orders emerge from what it terms the naturosphere. The fact that there is no absolute separation between the natural order and social orders, as will become clear, has far-reaching implications for the study of all social phenomena. For example, humans, the primary agents of society, are inextricably part of nature. [242]

Furthermore, energy is the major driving force of both nature and human economies (see Figure 1 and 2). The environment provides a range of resources without which economies and societies could not even exist, let alone flourish. Jevons identified energy extraction and production as the key drivers of industrial and economic progress. Morris views energy as a major influence on what he calls the shape of history. He defines social development as the ability of a society to 'get things done – to shape their physical, economic, social and intellectual environments to their own ends'. [243]

The Biomatrix is described as a 'web of systems that we observe in the universe....Systems thinking asserts that every system in the universe is co-produced or co-caused by other systems'. [244] The Biomatrix represents all systems in the universe, and has three major sub-webs: 'the naturosphere (i.e. nature's systems), psycho-sociosphere (i.e. psychological and social systems) and technosphere (technological systems). The psycho-sociosphere arises from the naturosphere....The psycho-sociosphere, in turn, gives rise to the technosphere, which comprises all the structures (artefacts) produced by individuals and societies both human and animal...'. [245]

The doctrine of a psycho-sociosphere emerging *from* the naturosphere, with the technosphere emerging, in turn, *from* the psycho-sociosphere, is consistent with the principle of antecedence in physics discussed in Chapter 9. Everything emerges from something pre-existing in the never-ending becoming of evolution. It is impossible to divorce nature and society.

In fact, Biomatrix theory places the naturosphere as the ontological foundation of all the universe's systems. This would suggest that the connection between natural and social orders is, indeed, fundamental. It may be asserted without fear of contradiction that it is impossible for human beings, and for the societies they create, to escape the effects of the laws of physics.

On a practical level, too, there are connections interwoven between nature and society. Increased scientific knowledge of nature, for example, has often led to leaps in technological and social progress, increasing control over nature, ultimately producing the technological civilisation we live in today. Applied sciences, from medicine to engineering, have enhanced the quality of social life.

Connections between nature and society may be found at all levels, biological, chemical, economic and technological. These examples support the Biomatrix principle that social systems *emerge from* the naturosphere. Human societies, emergent from various natural systems, do not stand outside the laws of causation and other natural laws. Furthermore, social phenomena are located in the space-time continuum as surely as are objects in nature. Space-time influences the operations of all systems. One example of this influence would be the entropic arrow of time. The laws of thermodynamics certainly apply to social systems as well as to nature: 'social organizations and entire human societies are not isolated systems. They, too, draw energy from their environments…the evolution of living things and human organization tends towards increasing structure and complexity, because energy is drawn from exogenous sources'. [246] Entropy, used in the general sense of dissolution of structure over time, is a colossal, on-going challenge to all systems.

Alongside Condorcet and Malthus, Herbert Spencer was one of the earliest social thinkers to draw parallels between nature and society. In his influential 1881 essay, *Progress: Its Law and Cause, with other Disquisitions*, he attempted to define a scientific law of progress. The result was an evolutionary theory of social development. Social progress, he wrote, follows exactly the same basic pattern of all organic growth, namely 'this same evolution of the simple into the complex, through successive differentiations…we shall find that the transformation of the homogeneous into the heterogeneous is that in which progress essentially consists'. [247] That is why he used the term 'social organism' to describe society. He conceived it to be an entity analogous to a living being. Spencer exemplified this organic principle of structured change at work on different levels of existence. [248]

Spencer concluded that an *a priori* evolutionary law lay behind these patterns of development in nature and society. He formulated this law as follows: 'Every active force produces more than one change – every cause produces more than one effect....Starting with the ultimate fact that every cause produces more than one effect, we may readily see that throughout creation there must have gone on, and must still go on, a never-ceasing transformation of the homogeneous into the heterogeneous.' [249] Society advances towards greater complexity through the multiple effects caused by the active, influential forces driving all growth. Just as in nature, there is competition in society to extract what he called 'nutriment' from the environment.

While Spencer developed his theory primarily through deductive logical argument, based on observed general similarities between evolution in nature and in society, Russian economist Nikolai D. Kondratieff used inductive inferences from detailed historical data to develop his theory of long economic waves. While Spencer's theory of universal evolutionary progress from simple to complex produces a linear shape, Kondratieff's wave theory is cyclical. Like Spencer, Condorcet had a linear vision of progress. For him, history was moving towards an end-point of perfect liberty and absolute knowledge. Malthus, by contrast, envisaged cycles of growth in society. The limits of natural resources, especially agricultural ones, constrained growth, causing cycles of development to turn downwards towards stagnation or decline as the balance between population growth and food production became lopsided.

Is the shape of history, then, predominantly linear or cyclical? Kondratieff's little 1935 masterpiece *The Long Waves in Economic Life* identified cyclical, wave-like patterns of economic life in capitalist systems which averaged fifty years in duration. In addition, he believed there were short waves of eighteen months to three years' duration, as well as intermediate waves of seven to eleven years. He defined regularity as repetition in recurring time intervals. He collected economic data from the US, UK and France from 1780 to the 1920s, a significant time span of around 140 years.

Kondratieff plotted a time series for changes to wholesale price levels, interest rates, wages, foreign trade and production and consumption indicators throughout this period. In each series, he noticed a succession of three waves, with each wave having an upswing lasting about twenty-five years, followed by a decline of slightly longer, or shorter, duration: 'The movements of the series which we have examined running from the end of the eighteenth century to the present time show long cycles…these waves have been shown with about the same timing in all the more important of the series examined.' [250] These recurrent patterns pointed to a definite cyclical process of economic development, the shaping forces of which are 'inherent in the essence of the capitalist economy'. [251]

Kondratieff's first long wave, from 1789–1849, showed a twenty-five year period of upswing to 1814 followed by economic decline and depression for thirty-five years, making a cycle of sixty years. The second wave, from 1849–1896, demonstrated a 'boom' of twenty-four years followed by a 'bust' of twenty-three years, yielding a shorter cycle of forty-seven years. The next upswing lasted twenty-four years until the 1920s which led, as everyone knows, to the time of the Great Depression in the 1930s. In each wave, there is a turning-point in economic fortunes, when the upswing ends and depression sets in. Eighty years later, the world experienced a huge 'bust' called the Great Recession which started in 2008. One suspects these economic waves first demonstrated by Kondratieff in the 1930s are still very much with us. They could be termed K-waves in honour of the man who discovered them.

Kondratieff noticed the following features of K- waves:

⬇ During depressions, agriculture undergoes a pronounced, lengthy setback.

⬇ Commodity prices reach their lowest level towards the end of a long wave.

⬇ Revolutions and wars tend to happen 'during the period of high tension in the expansion of economic forces'. [252]

⬆ On the positive side, recessions lead to 'an especially large number of important discoveries and inventions in the technique of production and communication, which, however, are usually applied on a large scale only at the beginning of the next long upswing'. [253]

The methods the Russian economist used are almost as important to the futurist as these insightful findings. Kondratieff collected and plotted economic data in several time-series over a period lasting just under a century and a half. He then constructed his hypothesis of long economic waves to interpret the recurrent patterns he had discovered. It is these periodic regularities which provide an empirical and logical basis for forecasts about the long-term behaviour of capitalist economies. Kondratieff argued that the data was sufficient 'to declare this cyclical character to be very probable'. [254]

Austrian economist Joseph Schumpeter (1883–1950), well-known for his theory of creative destruction in capitalist systems, built on Kondratieff's findings in his monumental two volume *Business Cycles*, published in 1939 following thirty years work on the concept. [255]

Cycles, Schumpeter explained, are part of the very essence of the organism which is behaving cyclically. [256] They are not simple phenomena, he warned, but constitute a process 'within which all elements of the economic system interact in certain characteristic ways'.[257] Like Kondratieff, he wanted to explain the underlying patterns of economic life.

Schumpeter began by analysing the properties of the system of prices and quantities of all goods and services, [258] fundamental to any economy. He then set out to monitor states of equilibrium and disequilibria within this system over time. He reasoned that the key factor in determining economic cycles was innovation. He described this phenomenon as 'the outstanding fact in the economic history of capitalist society…the basis of our model of the process of economic change'. [259] He termed the changes in the economic process brought about by innovation Economic Evolution. He defined it as 'the setting up of a new production function…a new commodity…[or] a new form of organization, such as a merger…[or] the opening up of new markets…'. [260]

Schumpeter was convinced that innovations cause disturbances, or disequilibria, in the economic production system by overturning the total cost curve of existing production. [261] New companies and new industries arise as a result of innovation and threaten the existence of older competitors and their products, prices and production systems.

Consequently, companies have lifespans just like people. Their reason for existence can be undermined by new products, new production techniques and new cost structures. The filing for bankruptcy of Eastman Kodak, once a global corporate giant, in January 2012, after 131 years of international business success, illustrates this principle. Schumpeter regarded what he termed the incessant rise and decay of firms and industries as a central feature of the economic processes of capitalism.

Typically, innovations cannot be absorbed smoothly. Instead, they disrupt the existing system, enforcing a 'distinct process of adaptation', during which some companies and their products and systems go under, while others survive or thrive. [262] For example, the invention of the motor car undermined the use of the horse and also took away the transportation dominance of the railways. Schumpeter cites the 'railroadization, the electrification and the motorization of the world' as prime instances of innovation. [263] Another example of an industrial innovation which had a transformative socio-economic impact was the production of oil, a key driver of economic progress for the whole of the twentieth century.

Schumpeter's concept of innovation illuminates the Kondratieff long wave theory which he acknowledged as an important discovery. Schumpeter identified the dominant innovation, or core technologies, of the first of the long waves (1787–1842) as the early breakthroughs of the industrial revolution, such as cotton innovations and construction of canals. The second wave (1843–1897) he characterised as the age of steam and steel. The third and final K-wave was propelled by electricity, motorisation and modern chemistry.

Due to the creative destruction of products and production models which are supplanted by innovations, Schumpeter concluded that economic and social progress cannot be said to proceed in a smooth, linear path: 'evolution is lopsided, discontinuous, disharmonious by nature... the history of capitalism is studded with violent bursts and catastrophes... evolution is a disturbance of existing structures and more like a series of explosions than a gentle, though incessant, transformation'. [264]

In addition to the bankruptcy of some companies during the process of creative destruction, there is also the 'painful process of readjustment of prices, quantities, and values as the contours of the new equilibrium system emerge'. [265]

A key aspect of Schumpeter's theory of Economic Evolution is the role of capital investment and credit in the development of innovations. Newly dominant technologies, and the growing industries they spawn, attract more credit and investment in their expansion phase. The monetary cycles of credit and debt accumulation, associated with the process of innovation, play an influential part in the peaks and troughs, booms and recessions, of the long economic waves first identified by Kondratieff. This is especially true when bank lending in this phase becomes over-exuberant and even reckless, and corporate and household debt reach unsustainable levels.

Schumpeter explained that money was not a commodity and was not subject to the restraining power of the supply-demand system. [266] This made it an inherently risky factor. The global credit crisis of 2008–2009 illustrates this risk side to 'free-floating' money. The volatile character of money is often highlighted in the behaviour of the stock market as well as rises and falls in the money markets: 'stock prices have more degrees of freedom than other prices...there is...much more scope for waves of optimism and pessimism on the stock exchange than there is in industrial and commercial business...'. [267]

When speculative bubbles burst, as they periodically do, and when debit levels rise too high, widespread economic decline can result. Looking at the Great Depression, Schumpeter noted a violent crash of the stock market as well as a very disordered monetary situation: 'Given the way in which both firms and households had run into debt during the twenties, it is clear that the accumulated load – in many cases, though not in all, very sensitive to a fall in price level – was instrumental in precipitating the depression.' [268] High debt levels also precipitated the Great Recession of 2008–2011.

Schumpeter points out that railroad construction during the upswing of the second long wave was financed by massive new credit and speculation, with railroad stocks peaking in 1852 then falling sharply in 1854. The age of railroad innovation, which revolutionised the economic order, was all but over by about 1860. [269]

In addition to the existence of these technological and monetary cycles in the capitalist system, there are also cyclical industries, such as those producing equipment and materials for use in times of prosperity, or for replacements at the end of the lifecycle of equipment. All of these factors influence the working of the cyclical mechanisms of Schumpeter's Economic Evolution.

Innovation, then, backed up by capital investment and credit, is the driving force of economic development. But in Schumpeter's universe it is a profoundly destabilising process. It leaves numerous bankrupt firms, as well as superannuated products and business models, in its wake. For these reasons, he believed that economic progress was cyclical, driven by incessant internal change, with the logic of boom years producing an inevitable bust or reversal of expansion a generation later. Recession, in this view, is the flip-side of innovation.

Kondratieff and Schumpeter showed with extensive data that there is a complex, internally generated cyclical process of economic evolution. Furthermore, the influence of K-waves on the social order on a global level is incontestable: 'Capitalism itself is, both in the economic and in the sociological sense, essentially one process, with the whole earth as its stage.' [270] Given the central role worldwide of the economy in the life of society, the theory of economic cycles effectively undermines the linear view of history marching towards progress.

But it isn't just economies which undergo recurrent cycles of development. One of America's most respected sociologists, Pitirim Sorokin, looked at the underlying dynamics of social evolution throughout the whole span of civilisational history. He defined the socio-cultural world as 'endless millions of individual objects, events, processes, fragments, having an infinite number of forms, properties and relationships'. [271] He discovered distinct patterns repeated throughout history.

Sorokin's doctrine of social change draws on a principle of the internal dynamic drivers of systems. Systems, that is, have their own built-in dynamics based on the fact that they are, by definition, whole functioning entities, made up of interconnected components, or variables, which each influence how the system as a whole behaves.

In particular, systems are unified by governing principles. Sorokin proposed a logico-meaningful approach to systems dynamics: 'Hidden behind the empirically different, seemingly unrelated fragments of the cultural complex lies an identity of meaning, which brings them together into consistent styles, typical forms and significant patterns.' [272] This meaning could be ideas or principles which 'logically integrate' a culture. [273] In any given culture, he argues, there is a logical connection between its variables and a 'dominant attitude toward the nature of ultimate reality'. [274] A prevailing worldview, system of truth and knowledge, or dominant mentality, underpins any logically integrated culture. It could be a 'super-sensory' mentality in religiously minded societies, or 'sensory' in more materialistic cultures. Cultures are unified by their underlying logic, values and principles.

Sorokin points out that change is radically different for cultures which are not logically integrated. 'Spatial congeries' are groups who happen to be in close proximity to one another without any cohesive sense of community or integrated culture. Social change works differently for these poorly integrated societies: 'In the congeries the change would mean mainly a mechanical addition or subtraction of elements, or their rearrangement chiefly through external forces....In the unified cultural systems the change would mean a transformation of the system as a whole or in its greater part.' [275]

He defines a society as a 'whole integrated culture...a constellation of many cultural subsystems' [276] which passes through states during its dynamic existence. It has a life career characterised by incessant fluctuations. Any socio-cultural system, he asserts, is a moulder of its own future. [277]

This is a basic principle for futurology. The greater the logical integration of a socio-cultural entity, the more change will be internally driven and transformative. On the other hand, less cohesive social entities ('congeries') will tend to be driven by changes brought about by external forces. [278] This principle forms part of Sorokin's doctrine of immanent self-regulation of systems. The more cohesive and integrated a society is, the less likely it is to experience internal disturbances and unrest during times of change. [279]

Strong systems will respond to future change in much more dynamic and positive ways than those which lack cohesion: 'Change in spatial congeries is almost always accidental. It does not have any inner logic and is the result of the interplay of various external factors....Any functional or logical system as a unity has a certain degree of autonomy and inherent self-regulation in its functioning and change....A cultural system has its own logic of function, change and destiny, which is a result not only (and regularly not so much) of the external conditions, but of its own nature.... Its life course is set down in its essentials when the system is born....At a certain point of its history (slightly accelerated or retarded by the external circumstances) the cultural system must undergo its inwardly ordained change.' [280]

The last two sentences are arresting. They indicate that a system's life course is internally pre-determined. A theory of the future is starting to emerge which draws on a quasi-deterministic view of the world. There is a significant degree of external and internal determinism built into the structure of reality.

Determinism, loosely defined, is the belief that all events happen in accordance with universal laws of nature and social development and that human beings cannot change the underlying structure of reality however hard they try. [281] By quasi-determinism, I mean there is some measure of free-will which allows humans the choice of actions within a narrow range of options presented by a largely pre-determined reality not of their own making. Sorokin himself believed in a form of self-determinism of social systems: 'Considering…that the determining potentialities of the system are the system itself and are its immanent properties, the determinism of the system turns into self-determinism. Self-determinism is the equivalent of freedom….The process of unfolding the immanent potentialities of the emerged system is somewhat predetermined by the system….Only the main direction and the main phases of the unfolding are predetermined.' [282] The greater the integration (including at the logical level of meaning and ethos), self-organisation and cohesiveness of a system, the less vulnerable it is to external forces and the higher the degree of self-determinism it enjoys. [283]

There is an opportunity during the lifespan of social systems for human leaders to intervene in shaping their evolution. Samet believes that human teleology, using foresight and design, and driven by defined purposes, decisively influences the evolution of social systems, along with external causes and immanent properties of systems. [284] He noted that teleology, or purposeful systems design, helps to distinguish social evolution from evolutionary biological processes.

Yet these interventions are ultimately dwarfed by recurrent patterns in social processes of change which Sorokin observed throughout history: 'The great symphony of social life is "scored" for a countless number of separate processes, each proceeding in a wavelike manner and recurring in space, in time, in both space and time, periodically or non-periodically, after short or long intervals….Economic processes fluctuate endlessly between prosperity and depression…vital processes between births, deaths, marriages, divorces; all undergo their "ups and downs" which sometimes become monotonously uniform. Crime and licentiousness, religion and irreligion, social stability and revolt, recur endlessly. Social systems… forever repeat the processes of recruiting, change, dismissal…originate, grow and dissolve. And so it goes with almost all social phenomena and process.' [285] The aim of sociology is to study scientifically these recurrent patterns of the socio-cultural process. [286]

Sorokin looked at the patterned fluctuations over a 2,500 year time-span. He analysed the influence of six main systems of truth which have underpinned human cultures in the history of the West. [287] Whitehead identified patterns of belief as one of the four elements of human civilisation, along with patterns of behaviour, patterns of emotion and technologies.

Sorokin found that none of his intellectual systems of truth have followed a linear progression, a fact that reinforces the case for a cyclical view of history. Each system, he argued, 'has fluctuated, now rising in its influence, now declining, or remaining for a time comparatively constant. [288] Whitehead spoke of general climates of opinion, like tidal movements, lasting two or three generations, within which there are shorter waves of thought. Fluctuations in influence of these six philosophical systems unfolded in time-spans from twenty to a thousand years: 'Frequently, they evidence a duration of about sixty or eighty, or even a hundred years.' [289] Yet these patterns of influence do not fluctuate in any mechanical or clockwork manner.

Sorokin also detected evidence of short-time oscillations within the longer waves. The former could only be understood in the context of the longer trends. He saw no Hegelian dialectic of thesis-antithesis-synthesis; rather, cultural history reveals a more complex, and, at times, erratic, story of overlapping short- and long-term trends of changing intellectual influence from the basic worldviews informing the ethos of societies.

In Sorokin's view, systems of truth, like other socio-cultural systems, are subject to trends caused immanently or internally, and all contain the seeds of their own future growth or decline, destined to follow the course of their pre-determined internal development. [290] For him, immanent change is the principal kind of change in socio-cultural systems, especially more integrated ones.

Historic cycles reflect systems dynamics as well as the way in which limits can bring about an end to periods of growth. Social processes *cannot* just keep going in one direction but invariably reach a limit at which point a change of direction occurs. In *The Collapse of Complex Societies* Tainter notes that collapse is a recurrent feature of human societies largely as a result of resource depletion, an important kind of limit. Limits that stop a society from growing could be these natural or external limits, including diminishing supplies of an important commodity or an environmental constraint such as soil degradation.

But limits can also be internal. For example, there are limits to the forms which socio-cultural entities can take : 'it is reasonably certain that an enormous number of sociocultural systems and processes have a limited range of possibilities in their variation, in the creation of new fundamental forms…after a sufficiently long existence of the process given, during which it runs through all the main forms, in its further existence it cannot help repeating the forms already used, either all of them, or some of them; either in the same order as before, or in a different order; but repetition and recurrence of the forms becomes inescapable under these conditions'. [291] The fewer forms the entity can take, the more its patterns of development will be highly regular and repetitive: 'the rhythm of the sociocultural process is in reverse relationship to the number of possible forms of its change'. [292]

There is a finite number of forms of government, so throughout history fluctuations will occur in which these kinds of government, such as democratic, totalitarian or oligarchic systems of power, increase or lose their influence in given societies. There is also a limited number of religions and philosophical worldviews which can determine a predominant system of truth for a society.

Let us take the evolution of such a system of truth as an example of how internal limits shape the destiny of a society: 'No creed is exempt from…conflicts of interpretations, dogmas and principles, though they all claim to be the truths of faith. As a result, it is only a matter of time before they begin their mutual struggle and are forced to resort to reason, logic, and sensory experience to prove the point of each faction. These circumstances and tendencies show that the truth of faith has also a limit in its development and domination and immanently calls forth its own decline for some period of time….All forms of truth are subject to this "dialectical destiny" and are hardly exempt from a self-preparation of their own decline in the course of their development.' [293]

Sorokin claimed that this rise and fall of systems of truth from dominance to decline is a never-ending process which would continue to fluctuate, or rise and fall, as long as human society existed. This was due to the fact that the fluctuations arose from the very nature of these systems of truth: 'Perhaps the deepest reason for such a fluctuation is that none of these…systems of truth contains the whole truth, the truth of a really omniscient mind. Each of them has, perhaps, only a part of truth and side by side with it a part of falsity. When the falsity begins to take the upper hand over the truth the system has, it begins to decline and the other forms of truth accentuate that part of the Whole Truth which was deficient in the preceding system. Then in its turn it repeats the same "cycle".' [294]

This is all positive news for the social scientist. Empirically observed recurrent patterns, or cycles, of evolution provide grounds for foreknowledge. Over time, repeated patterns occur as social systems undergo changes in form, or transformations. Once they have exhausted all available forms, there will be a re-emergence of an old form, perhaps in a new guise. This process causes cyclical recurrence of patterns of development.

Contemporary historian Ian Morris has also noted that the concept of limits can produce recurrent cycles of development. He coined the term the 'paradox of development' to describe the phenomenon that use of resources to generate social development can overshoot and undermine subsequent development. Development, in other words, can produce ceilings which block further progress. Transcendence of these historic ceilings requires some sort of transformative change. If societies fail to transform at this point, they begin to decline, leading eventually to possible state failure.

Sorokin's twin principles of immanent change of systems, and his concept of limits, account together for the cyclical rhythms and recurrent patterns in his doctrine of social evolution. [295] The identification of recurrent fluctuations, or alternating increases and decreases, in the intellectual life of humanity, and in the prevailing mentalities of culture, is a major finding in the search for the laws of social evolution.

Causes of social change are to be found mostly within the internal properties of these social systems to a much greater extent than the influence of external factors in the environment. This is not to say external factors are irrelevant, only that they are secondary.

The patterns of intellectual and philosophical trends in social history are important for studying, and predicting, social behaviour. Morris believes he has identified laws of history in the same way in which Sorokin has accumulated evidence of the existence of sociological laws operating throughout the development of civilisation. Morris explains how social development takes place across history by using three key principles from biology, sociology and geography.

Geography determines what resources are made available to any given group of people. This aspect can be illustrated by looking at the rise of Rome in history: 'In Rome's empire, ninety percent of the people lived within ten miles of the Mediterranean Sea.' [296] The early Romans had access to great rivers and seas for trade. This enabled them to expand commercially and politically. The location of a society determines the scope for its early advancement. Eventually, that development alters the geography: 'social development changes what geography means.... Geography determined where in the world social development would rise fastest, but rising development changed what geography meant.'[297] This principle shows once again the reciprocal nature of the relationship between nature and society.

Regarding the sociological dimension of development, Morris argues that societies develop primarily by harnessing energy. Their survival and prosperity are dependent on extracting energy from the environment and then capturing, and using, it. Humans have always fed off the 'Great Chain of Energy' [298] stretching from the sun to the plants and animals eaten for food.

Between 7000 and 5000 BC foragers turned into pastoralists when they domesticated wild cattle and sheep, gaining decisive social advantages over nomadic peoples. Those who farmed, Morris explains, captured more energy from earth than those who did not. So they developed faster.

Morris locates the root of most social change in biology: 'Change is caused by lazy, greedy, frightened people looking for easier, more profitable, and safer ways to do things.' [299] This statement implies that human behaviour is driven, almost involuntarily, by the biological need to live securely, that is, to survive, and, once that aim has been achieved, to prosper in the environment in order to make life easier. Schumpeter also identified the meaning of economic activity as the satisfaction of human wants. [300] So societies and economies develop from the systems devised by humans to enable them to prosper – live more easily – in their given geographies.

Futurists neglect the influence of humanity's biologically-based behaviour at their peril. In *Physics of the Future* Kaku has developed what he calls the Cave Man Principle, arguing that human wants, dreams and desires have not changed in 100,000 years. Kaku argues that these universal needs always trump technology if the latter conflicts with, or contradicts, the former. He cites a never-ending conflict between High Tech (e.g. watching TV) and High Touch (e.g. going to a live sports event), concluding that, given a straight choice between these two kinds of experience, other factors being equal, Cave Man and Cave Woman will invariably choose High Touch.

Morris is as certain as Kaku that universal principles, from biology, sociology and geography, underlie the whole spread of history: 'these biological and sociological laws are constants, applying everywhere, in all times and all places'. [301] The social sciences, he says, seek to explain what causes social change: 'behind all the details of what has happened in the last fifteen thousand years, two sets of laws – those of biology and sociology – determined the shape of history on a global scale, while a third set – those of geography – determined the differences between Eastern and Western development....'. [302]

There is a common thread running through the theories of Kondratieff, Schumpeter, Sorokin and Morris. They reveal the presence in history of economic, social, cultural and intellectual waves, or cycles of development, over truly enormous expanses of time. These thinkers conclude that the never-ending cyclical processes have resulted from internal dynamics of social systems designed for the satisfaction of the human need to survive and develop.

The processes of change, in other words, are driven by a logic within the systems themselves, whether they be systems of truth, systems of economic production or socio-cultural systems. They are driven by societies wanting to make life easier and better. The endless cycles of development result from a dynamic of progress of overcoming, or being overcome by, limits. Progress brings human beings up against limits, both external and internal, causing growth to slow. At this point the wave of development dips towards decline. Then some innovation is typically discovered to stimulate new means of wealth creation and social development and a new cycle begins. Limits always need to be transcended – hence the fundamental role of innovation as shown in Schumpeter's theory of economic history.

We have arrived at another milestone in the theory of foreknowledge. Social evolution is a cyclical process built into the very fabric of social orders and systems in a way analogous to laws of nature. Just as there are endlessly recurrent processes in the world of physics, so there are long waves of intellectual and cultural history, as well as proven K-waves in capitalist economies.

This indicates that social life is far from unpredictable. Existing scientific knowledge, including within the body of social sciences, provides a bridge for inferential knowledge of the social future. It is incontestable that cycles of social change demonstrated over titanic periods of time provide a logical basis for long-range forecasts of the social future.

Ultimately, it is time, not money, that makes the world go round.

CHAPTER 12
SEEING INTO THE FAR FUTURE

The establishment of an epistemology of foreknowledge would inaugurate a race to produce real knowledge of the world's future. The scope of such foreknowledge could be expansive, including the far future. Complexity scientist Robert Samet, for example, has constructed a model of long-range futures research which adopts a planning time horizon of 100–150 years to 2150 but an evolutionary 'deep future' trajectory to as far ahead as 2250. [303]

Samet proposes an evolutionary approach to understanding the long-term future of civilisations: 'The evolution of civilisation involves irreversible and continuing changes over time, which creates long-term development and disequilibrium with increasing diversity, specialisation, connectivity, and complexity in the world system of cities.' [304]

He distinguishes between foresight, required for near-term and medium-term planning, and prescience, which is evolutionary foreknowledge. The purpose of prescience is 'to explain past evolution and explore potential futures.' [305] Samet also highlights the difference between extrapolation, a technique for researching the near-future based on current realities, and prognostication, which is used for long-range futures research where there is a scientific basis for understanding the projected future of a social system.

In Chapter 9, the ubiquity of lifecycles, or patterns of development within a lifespan, was noted. Then the previous chapter illustrated how they operate in social history. Phenomena may be located on a timeline showing past-evolution, present state and anticipated future-evolution. This kind of evolutionary long-range analysis is what produces prognostication.

Samet develops the following classification for futurological research:

↑ Projective forecasts derived from trend analysis with time horizons to ten years.

↑Prospective research using scenarios, and longer-term scenario modeling, [306] with a time horizon of twenty-five to fifty years.

↑Evolutionary future research on spatial structures for long-range horizons up to 125 years, based on gradual adaptation of social systems to their environment.

It is the last category of future research which has the most relevance for an empirical epistemology of the future developed in this study.

Samet clarifies various crucial long-term evolutionary time-scales: 'The metacycles of astrophysical and geophysical time are measured in billions of years, biological evolutionary timescales are measured in millions of years, with humankind emerging five million years ago. Deep futures involve scientific speculation on the future of life on the planet Earth a million years or more into the future. The civil metacycle…is measured in units of millennia, and a possible starting point for civilisation was fifty millennia ago….The megacycles for the evolution of cities are also measured in millennia, in relation to macrocycles of a century or less for the life of buildings, establishments, technological, and human life cycles.' [307]

The above time-scales are an essential dimension of future knowledge. Russell stressed the need to specify the 'when' of the future as precisely as possible. It has been a central theme of this work that the future is a form of time. Understanding the future involves a conceptualisation of time. It has further been suggested that time is an evolutionary medium. Time-cycles allow the futurist to plot evolutionary trajectories into the long-term future.

A fairly recent intellectual discovery has clarified a mathematical method for predicting the future time-span of any given entity, whether an organism, a building, an organisation or even a civilisation. The method shows in a very concrete fashion the power of understanding how time, and its cycles, work. This new approach is of considerable value to the discipline of futurology, which must aspire to be as temporally precise as possible. This discovery is called the Copernican Principle.

In 1969, astrophysicist J. Richard Gott was visiting the Berlin Wall. Gott wondered how long the menacing wall would remain in place. His scientific training told him that Copernicus had shown that earth did not occupy a special position in the solar system. It was logical to extend this argument, he thought, to the idea that no location anywhere in space or in time is ever special. 'If there was nothing special about the location of my visit in time, there was a fifty percent chance that I was observing the wall sometime during the middle two quarters of its existence....So standing at the wall in 1969, I predicted...that there was a fifty percent chance that the future longevity of the wall would be between two and two-third years and twenty-four years....When the wall came down in 1989, after twenty years, in agreement with my original prediction, I decided that I should write this up.' [308]

Gott's principle is that we observe things at random, i.e. non-special, times so that there is always a fifty percent chance that we are doing so in the middle of their lifespan. So, if we divide up an entity's lifespan into four quarters, there is a twenty-five percent chance that we are observing it in the first quarter, a fifty percent chance of witnessing it in the middle two quarters and a twenty-five percent chance of watching it in the final quarter of its existence. You just have to find out its start date, as Gott did when he visited that oppressive symbol of the Cold War.

In addition, Gott has shown that things which have lasted a long time already will tend to be around for a long time to come, while things of short duration will probably not last very long. All of this shows the crucial importance of a proper sense of time scale. It is the past-evolution of entities which forms the basis for predicting their future-evolution: 'In general, use time past to predict time future, and use the number of people in the past to predict the number of people in the future.' [309]

Gott has come up with a smart way of estimating the future duration of entities we observe, once again showing how existing knowledge (the Copernican system) can become a platform for new knowledge (the Copernican, or Gott, Principle). After Einstein, we have reasoned, there is no need to see time as a mystery or the future as some kind of dark, uncharted territory. What we need in foreknowledge is a proper sense of time-scales and the way in which entities behave within these periods of time.

In the same way that futurists typically integrate insights from multiple disciplines, from economics to environmental science, from psychology to sociology, so it should be a standard futurological practice to compare time-scales for these dimensions as part of the process of integrating knowledge across fields of enquiry: 'The long-term goal for civilisations is to achieve a dynamic balance between a growing human population, the astrophysical systems of the Earth and the Sun, and the terrestrial stocks of the geophysical system.' [311] Samet is correct in stressing that the long-term goal of civilisation is maintaining a balance between nature and society. It is probable that the coming generations will belong to an Ecological Age, following the end of the Age of Fossil Fuels after the threatening sequence of Peak Oil, Peak Coal and Peak Gas takes place in this century.

A futurist will look at lifecycles in the terrestrial stocks, such as oil and arable land, and map them against demographic projections for future global population levels. He or she will also look at the energy demands of social technologies compared to actual finite terrestrial stocks. This is part of the trans-disciplinary integration of knowledge. A futurist must integrate measurements of time and spatial factors in keeping with the fundamental doctrine established by Einstein of the space-time continuum.

Samet's long-range civilisational goal, stated above, is an effective paradigm for futurists to bear in mind when making social forecasts integrating analysis of relevant time-cycles in nature and in social systems. Those studying the potential impacts of climate change, for example, need to look at impacts on socio-economic and technological development of rising temperatures over specific time periods.

It's the behaviour of entities in, and through, time that counts. They all have lifespans. Their typical patterns of development become evident over these spans of time, including vast tracts of historical time, as well as durations in evolutionary deep time, which are scarcely conceivable by the human mind. Now that time has been decisively demystified and thinkers like Samet have succeeded in mapping out the time scales of the future, we are no longer overawed by time. It falls squarely within the range of our understanding. The race to know the future has begun.

CHAPTER 13
IS POLITICS PREDICTABLY UNPREDICTABLE?

The race to know our future faces one final roadblock. It is the problem of the apparent unpredictablity of politics, a dimension of social life with power to effect large-scale change. You may well be wondering whether politics could ever be predictable enough for us to gain foreknowledge in this influential area of human endeavour.

Turn on any of the satellite global TV news channels. You will see plenty of examples of political turmoil around the world: terrorism, unrest, revolutions, riots, coups, corruption, scandals, government bankruptcies and the like. If politics is such a fertile source of disorder, how realistic is the belief that humanity can gain foreknowledge of our future? Will we ever get a better handle on our destiny through knowledge of the political future? Isn't politics always going to be a volatile field of enquiry, ultimately beyond our ability to fully understand and foreknow? Is the unpredictability of politics reality or myth?

A multi-dimensional analysis of H.G. Wells' predictions in his futuristic work *Anticipations* revealed a low score for his political forecasts (see Table 2 in Chapter 4). In this field, he attained a poor success rate of ten percent. Four out of his five political predictions proved to be incorrect. They were underpinned by ideologically biased theory. He performed better in his technological, economic and social forecasts.

Condorcet was more politically prescient than Wells. The French prognostic thinker predicted the rise of women's rights almost a hundred years in advance, perhaps the greatest social prediction of all time (see Appendix 1). It does seem true, nevertheless, that it is especially difficult to produce accurate political forecasts. And, on the face of it, it looks like there is substantial scope for political turbulence in the century ahead. The global structure of current nation-states overlays shifting demographic 'tectonic plates' which are no respecter of these national barriers, as Samet has shown: 'The United Nations now officially recognises nearly 200 countries or nation-states, compared with only seventy-two states and colonies in 1945, although these states assert sovereignty over some 5,000 ethnic groups whose occupation of their homeland predates the birth of the state…some two-thirds of states use military force or intimidation and human rights violations against people they claim as citizens.….The majority of existing nation-states have been created by the consolidation of occupied territories, when a more powerful nation has formed a colony or an empire.' [311] Samet shows here that the global structure of nation-states may well be built on shifting sand, not rock.

Another example of a discontinuity between the surface reality of nation-states and the underlying tectonics of shifting social and ethnic groupings is the disjunction between the 105 state languages of nation-states compared to the 6,000 or more living languages.

There are, then, significant fault-lines in the geo-political landscape. They virtually guarantee a long series of political earthquakes, tremors and after-shocks in the twenty-first century. The potential for the horrors of ethnic cleansing and religious persecution, as witnessed in the Bosnian conflict in the 1990s, looms over our current century like a long black cloud.

In Communist China, for example, which presents a monolithic nation-state front to the world, there are 60 million Muslims, whose religion is being suppressed, not to mention millions of Christians, who are also being persecuted. [312] There are ethnic, religious and racial dynamics which simply do not fit inside the box of 'global nation-state' as it is currently configured. Consequently, major socio-political change lies ahead. Samet predicts the emergence of around 1,000 ecopolitan, or highly localised, states out of our current 200 nation-states, by the year 2150. [313] The modern era of the nation-state, which began with revolution in France and America, is about to enter a protracted period of devolution. Such devolution will entail massive political changes, creating significant potential for conflict in the decades ahead.

Exacerbating this threat of tectonic political shifts is the scenario of increased scarcity of resources and corresponding rising prices for key commodities. There are declining oil supplies, relative to escalating global demand. There is water and food scarcity in some regions. There is concern about China's growing global monopoly of vital rare earth elements.

Given the difficulties of political forecasting and a twenty-first century political landscape with deep fault-lines, which could engender sustained levels of change and instability throughout the century, what are the realistic chances of building up accurate political foreknowledge?

A week in politics may, indeed, be a long time, as former British Prime Minister Harold Wilson (1916–95), once quipped. Equally, though, there is a long time in a week. Put another way, each week in politics carries the weight of human history. The long waves of history, all the cycles of economic, social and cultural development, continue to roll on as leaders come and go on the world stage. Adolf Hitler's Thousand Year Reich, despite the almost superhuman will he imposed on events during his rule, lasted all of eleven years. This was a whopping 989 years short of the time-span of his thousand-year dream.

What are the so-called supermen of history compared to super-history? There is destiny built into time. There are purposes of the great force of time. Spengler, the renowned German philospher of history coined the phrase 'the philosophy of destiny'. [314] Economic factors like a country's energy use, its natural resources, the health of its currency, its employment rate, its farming and food production, its trade relations – these factors dwarf the role of politicians, even charismatic demagogues. International factors, especially trade, ultimately overshadow national ones.

Spengler defined politics as the form in which the history of a nation is accomplished within a plurality of nations. [315] In the grand historical perspective, a nation's future 'will be decided by its force-relationships towards other peoples and powers and not by its mere internal ordering.' [316] It is interesting that he placed foreign relations at a higher level of priority than domestic politics.

A sense of history and a sense of the future – these are pre-requisites for visionary political leadership. The great political leader is a servant of history and of Spengler's destiny (which we could call 'super-history').

Political leaders, ultimately, are servants of the systems they inherit, including global systems to which their nations are connected. They are mere participants in the unfolding of super-history. As a result, there are many more variables in political decision-making over which they have no control than there are variables which they do control. The current school of thought called Big History focuses on patterns of change on vast scales of time, including cosmological. No doubt Spengler is smiling in his grave.

Hitler's extreme policies violated laws of history, religion, morality, politics and nature. That is why his fall was as spectacular as his brutal ascent to power had been. Part of the human understanding of time is thus to develop a sense of history and of destiny while cultivating a humble spirit before the immensities of space and time around us. There is a logic of time that is greater than all of our lives. History is destiny.

One contemporary thinker who believes that politics, and politicians, are actually quite predictable is Bruce Bueno de Mesquita, political scholar at New York University and author of *The Predictioneer's Game.* He believes this not so much because of the idea of a 'super-history', with its long-term trends and laws, but because human-decision-making is inherently, predictably, self-interested. De Mesquita applies the principles of game theory to predict the likely outcomes of decision-making processes, especially in politics. He explains: 'Politics is predictable....The key to good prediction is getting the logic right....Prediction with game theory requires learning how to think strategically about other people's problems the way you think about your own.' [317] The essence of game theory is the idea 'that people do what they believe is in their best interest....By estimating carefully people's wants and beliefs, anyone can make a reliable forecast of what each and every one of them will do'. [318] People, that is, have a survival instinct. They behave strategically. They act rationally in their own self-interest: 'Rationality is about choosing actions that are consistent with advancing personal interests....Taking calculated risks is part of being rational. I just need to think about the size of the risk, the value of the reward that comes with success, and the cost that comes with failure, and compare those to the risks, costs and benefits of doing things differently.' [319]

In short, de Mesquita claims people, especially politicians, are predictably rational and self-interested: 'Since everyone involved in a given problem is concerned with getting what they want, their behaviour and choices are predictable....Once an issue is properly framed, we have to think about how to capture the thought process that people go through in working out decisions.' [320]

Hawking has identified two reasons why social behaviour is not as predictable as behaviour in nature, namely, (i) irrational and/or incorrect decision-making and (ii) incomplete decision-making. [321] Whilst human decision-making is often incorrect and incomplete, it is a moot point whether irrationality is as significant a factor as Hawking here suggests. We have seen that game theorists, for example, see humans as agents who always act rationally and strategically to advance their own interests. [322]

The application of game theory to political decision-making seems to be a successful model. It has led to a high rate of correct predictions. But political events and states are not just about decision-making. They are also about deeper conditions rooted in history, including patterns of long-term evolutionary change. Decision-making might occur at the surface of events, but there are complex background factors which are rooted in the deep past.

I do not see human behaviour as unpredictable at either the social or political levels. Sorokin showed that in times of social crisis and social anxiety, for example, a law of polarisation works: 'Some…are turned into pure eternalists who try to anchor human existence to something solid, lasting, capable of withstanding all the storms of the empirical reality; others are turned into the extreme sensual temporalists of the *carpe diem* type…we have met and shall meet his law of polarization several times. It seems to be of a fairly general nature.'[323] There are numerous such examples of predictable human behaviour under a variety of social conditions which have been observed by sociologists and historians alike.

Chapter 11 established beyond a reasonable doubt that there are deep structures to history, driving forces in society, culture and in the economy which are responsible for the long-term cycles of social change. If politics is, indeed, predictable at both the surface and deep structure level, then it will turn out to be as quasi-determined as the rest of reality. Case studies of long-range social forecasts by the likes of Condorcet and H.G. Wells, and correct contemporary predictions of short-term political decision-making by de Mesquita, have demonstrated in practice that it is possible to predict social development and human behaviour.

Politics, then, is no island. It occurs, like everything else, within space-time. It is connected with the Biomatrix to other social and natural systems. It is part of evolving history. These contexts influence and constrain the behaviour of politicians and political groups, taming the apparent unpredictability of politics.

In returning to the real drivers of socio-political development, we can close this chapter by showing how political power cannot be divorced from economic power: 'we can distinguish between two systems of power, the political system and the economic system. The former consists in principle of elected representatives of the people who set public policy; the latter, in principle, is a system of private power…free from public control…the centers of private power exert an inordinately heavy influence…through control of the media, through control of political organizations….Roughly speaking, I think it's accurate to say that a corporate elite of managers and owners governs the economy and the political system as well – at least in a very large measure.' [324] Power, especially financial and economic power, has always been the essence of politics.

Whether one agrees with Chomsky's assertion here or not, it is certainly true that one cannot separate politics from economics or from the financial systems of a country, just as one cannot divorce economics from society or, indeed, from nature itself in the tightly interconnected Biomatrix web. Any argument that politics is unpredictable when foreknowledge of nature, society, culture, history and the economy can be gained through applying the laws and principles of social evolution, is not going to hold up. Political systems, in this context, are never isolated.

CHAPTER 14
THE SEARCH FOR OUR FUTURE

The future's unpredictability has been greatly exaggerated, even in the seemingly uncertain areas of life such as politics. The search for our future is yielding positive results. Social progress to date has focused largely on the conquest of space through material development. It is astonishing that we have been overawed by the mystery of time, especially the future, for so long. We have struggled all along to understand, study and leverage the future.

Yet space and time form one 4D continiuum as the reality in which we exist. So progress which is limited to spatial expansion and development must fail to optimise our mastery of the world. The conquest of time is still in its infancy despite the fact that the future is an asset we desperately need to commandeer. The story of our search for a science of the future, led by pioneers of prognostic thinking like Condorcet, Malthus, Jevons and H. G. Wells, is an unfinished one.

In the past, people have tended to adopt either an optimistic or a pessimistic outlook on the future. But both approaches suffer from vagueness. The scientific view of time, in contrast, is much more precise and will prove far more beneficial to society.

Time does not permit us the luxury of optimism. The law of entropy ensures that. Condorcet's idealistic picture of the future of society in which slavery and oppression of women would officially end proved accurate – in part. Not all forms of slavery have ended. Human trafficking is still a major global problem. Nor do women have voting rights in all countries. Abuse of women and children is rife in the world.

Nor is pessimism likely to yield a true picture of the future. Time is an evolutionary medium. Over the long-term societies evolve, sometimes in accelerated periods of development. Malthus' doomsday scenarios of mass starvation in Britain did not come to pass, even though his words of caution about the risks of over-population do echo down the centuries.

Optimism and pessimism both reflect a mood, attitude or thought climate, rather than an objective, fact-based understanding of how time works. Instead of optimism or pessimism, a more realistic, scientific approach to the future, which respects the nature of time as well as the multi-dimensional nature of reality, seems to be the most effective outlook. It is time to transcend the age-old dichotomy of optimism or pessimism and employ a more proactive, objective mindset. Optimism and pessimism are both *so* twentieth century.

Let us look at how the outmoded approaches of optimism and pessimism can colour analysis of the future, skewing the resulting prognostications. In 1967, just before the successful Apollo 11 moon mission, futurists Herman Kahn and Anthony Wiener published a book entitled *The Year 2000* with the descriptive sub-title *A Framework for Speculation on the Next Thirty-Three Years*. The authors based their projections on 'gross, long-term trends'. [325] (Incidentally, Herman Kahn was the futurist from the Rand Corporation who was caricatured in Stanley Kubrick's 1964 black comedy *Dr. Strangelove or: How I Learned to Stop Worrying and Love the Bomb*. The character representing Kahn was played by Peter Sellers.)

Kahn and Wiener tabled thirteen long-term trends of Western society present over several centuries. These trends included the spread of western-style secular humanism, the institutionalisation of scientific and technological innovation in research and development divisions and what they called the 'expectation of continuous economic growth'. [326] The last statement reveals their optimism. The authors extrapolated these thirteen trends [327] over the chosen future time horizon of three decades, but in their optimism they exaggerated certain trends while underestimating the impact of limits to growth.

Underlying their thirteen developments are key quantifiable variables such as population growth, literacy, gross national product, energy sources, military strength, and so on. Kahn and Wiener defined key variables as those factors which constrain 'the possibilities for any society'. [328]

The authors described a baseline 'standard world' picture of the future. Variations were then built around this standard world according to variables and issues which were considered likely to be influential in this future time period. The variations to the 'standard world' were divided into three categories depending on possible influences of variables such as the arms race/arms control issue and whether the world would become more A. Integrated, B. Inward-looking or C. Chaotic. The determining criterion for these three categories was seen as the degree of political consultation and peace, including arms control, prevailing between the ten dominant countries they identified. Depending on the level of political peace and global coordination that could be attained, their standard world picture was pushed in the direction of either greater disarray or integration. Using this methodology, they devised a very sophisticated set of global scenarios to the Year 2000.

The authors defined scenarios as 'hypothetical sequences of events constructed for the purpose of focusing attention on causal processes and decision-points'. [329] They also used 'alternative futures' to provide systematic comparisons of alternative policies, or combinations of assumptions, objectives and issues. [330] In futurological models like this, it is important to make assumptions explicit and to illustrate how specific issues can affect future events. [331] It is notable that they chose the thirteen trends after analysis of theoretical principles of long-term historical change. [332]

For the purposes of this case study, several examples of general and specific forecasts will be evaluated, using the same dimensions applied to the study of the predictions of H.G. Wells in chapter 4.

Table 3 Survey of Year 2000 predictions

Prediction	Primary dimension	Accuracy	Theoretical soundness	Theoretical implications
1. '[E]xtensive and worldwide use of high altitude cameras for mapping, prospecting, census, land use and geological investigations'	Technological	Correct ✓	Generally sound; even anticipates Google Earth kind of applications of high altitude mapping	Once a technology is available and economical to use, futurists should anticipate its possible uses in different dimensions and sectors of society
2. '[R]elatively effective appetite and weight control'	Social	Incorrect ☒ There is a huge world-wide obesity health problem	Over-estimated capacity of public to use increased health knowledge to change lifestyle choices	Difficulty in changing human behaviour just with knowledge or technology when short-term interests are affected
3. '[E]xtensive use of robots and machine's "slaved" to humans'; robotics used for 'automated or more mechanised housekeeping and home maintenance'	Technology	Incorrect ☒	Partially sound; underestimated the pivotal role of consumer adoption of domestic robots	Consumer choice difficult to predict; aesthetic and ethical dimensions of human choice of technology need to be factored in
4. '[S]ome control of weather and/or climate'	Technology	Incorrect ☒ Control of climate has decreased through climate change	Unsound; over-estimated human control of nature; under-estimated power of nature; did not foresee climate change	Avoid **technological optimism**; rather, factor in complexity of technology cycles; avoid fallacy of human control over nature; rather, factor in complexity of natural systems

5. '[P]ermanent manned satellite and lunar installations' and inter-planetary travel	Technological	Partially correct ✓ ☒, There is a permanently manned space station but no lunar installations are likely in the foreseeable future	Partially sound; technological capability on its own is not a sufficient condition for its deployment, especially in extreme scenarios	Avoid technological optimism: factor in cost and cost-to-benefit factors and viability of extreme technology scenarios
6. '[P]ermanent inhabited undersea installations and perhaps even colonies'	Technological	Incorrect ☒ No such undersea colonies exist nor are there any well-developed plans to build any	Partially sound; technology capability on its own is not a sufficient condition for its deployment, especially in extreme scenarios	Avoid technological optimism and 'novelty amplification effect'; factor in cost and cost-to-benefit factors and viability of extreme technology scenarios
7. '[U]nexpensive worldwide transportation of humans and cargo' and 'inexpensive road-free transportation', plus 'very low-cost buildings for home and business use'	Economic	Incorrect ☒ Transportation costs continue to rise steeply especially due to rising energy costs	Unsound; underestimates the rising demand and diminishing supply of key energy sources like fossil fuels, especially oil	Include economic analysis of energy behind the transport technology in transportation forecasts; underestimated rising costs and cost pressures due to energy cycles
8. Predicted 'ten 'major' powers of which two, the US and USSR, would be superpowers. Japan, West Germany, France, China, and the UK would be large powers; India, Italy, and Canada intermediate powers; the rest being small powers.	Political	Incorrect ☒; They did not foresee the collapse of the USSR in this time period, and the resultant uni-polar structure with one superpower; they underestimated the rise of China; did not foresee the loss of Japan's economic prowess and influence; they neglected the oil-rich Arab bloc; did not foresee the reunification of Germany	Partially sound; Did not understand contrasting economic and social dynamics of capitalism and communism, democracy versus state control, leading to blind spot about continued super-power status of USSR	State difficulty of political forecasts due to increased unpredictability; factor in dynamics of competing political economies to long-range political forecasts; factor in resource analysis, including geopolitical influence of energy resources

9. The authors predicted the development of regional power blocs: North America, a European bloc, African bloc, Arab bloc, Indian bloc, Chinese bloc	Political	Correct ✓	Factor in integrating factors versus polarizing factors in geopolitical forecasts; economic interests, cultural factors and geopolitical strategies are key
10. 'Automated, universal (real time) credit, audit and banking systems'	Technology	Correct ✓	Technology capability stands the cost-to-benefit test for applicability; influence of economic globalisation on financial services factored in
11. '[S]imple inexpensive home video recording and playing' and 'direct broadcasts from satellites to home receivers'	Technology	Correct ✓	Technology capability matched with ready global consumer acceptance to create mass scale adoption
12. 'Three-dimensional photography, illustrations, movies and television' widespread use of holography in 3-D television and motion pictures	Technology	Correct ✓ There is rising popularity of 3-D movies and television	Technology capability matched with ready global consumer acceptance to create mass scale adoption
13. '[P]ervasive business use of computers' and 'home computers to "run" household and communicate with outside world'	Technology	Correct ✓	Technology capability matched with ready global consumer acceptance to create mass scale adoption

Forecast	Category	Assessment	Soundness	Recommendation
14. Forecasts sharp decline in deaths by heart failure and cancer ('the cure rate, currently about one-third of the cases, is expected to double by the close of the century')	Technology	Incorrect ☒	Unsound; under-estimated growth of lifestyle health problems arising from consumerism	Balance influence of lifestyle and other factors of human behaviour with technology advancements
15. '[T]he next thirty-three years may well be known as the age of electronics, computers, automation, cybernation, data processing, or some related idea.'	Technology	Correct ✓ They correctly identified the dominant driving technology for the time period of the forecast	Sound	Technology capability matched with ready global consumer acceptance to create mass scale adoption
16. 'By the year 2000, computers are likely to match, stimulate, or surpass some of man's most "human-like" intellectual abilities, including perhaps some of his aesthetic and creative capacities, in addition to having some kinds of capabilities that human beings do not have.' Computer intelligence, they argued, would exceed human intelligence: 'in particular, as computers become more self-programming they will increasingly tend to perform activities that amount to "learning" from experience and training.'	Technology	Incorrect ✓ Computers are still glorified processors and do not have anything like human intelligence or the ability to self-learn or self-program'.	Partially sound; They overestimated how far the computer revolution would extend.	Avoid technological optimism and 'novelty amplification effect'; assess the true capabilities of human consciousness and the scientific ability to replicate human consciousness

Table 3 indicates roughly a fifty/fifty forecasting record of accuracy, with eight incorrect, seven correct and one partially correct score. It is clear that a general economic and technological optimism pervades the Year 2000 prognostications. This led to several false inferences. The authors erred on the side of optimism. The problem of optimism is its vagueness, allowing subjective exaggeration to take place.

Futurists need to avoid what may be called the trap of the self-amplifying present whereby current paradigms are assumed to continue without interruption into the future and to enjoy unlimited growth, ignoring the role of cycles in social evolution. In my view, the cyclical nature of social evolution has been proved beyond a reasonable doubt (see Chapter 11). Linear projections of trends are bound to run afoul of this evolutionary law at some stage. This is why futurist cannot be optimists.

The Year 2000 authors were caught up in what they acknowledged was the speeding up of economic growth in their world at the time. They were naïve about the nature of time. They were caught in the trap of the self-amplifying present.

Kahn and Wiener cited four causes for this global spurt in growth and their own 'optimistic bias'[333]: (a) the commitment of an increasing number of countries to policies of economic expansion; (b) an exponentially growing body of technical knowledge, including management science, which would lead to increased productivity or a 'multiplication of productive powers';[334] (c) the smoothing out of depressions through use of government deficits (i.e. borrowing); and (d) improvements in 'world institutional arrangements'.[335]

With the benefit of hindsight, it is possible to look back on the 2008 global credit crisis and ensuing worldwide recession, followed by the euro zone crisis, as evidence that government borrowing, and excessive debt in general, can derail economic growth, especially in an era of rising energy costs. The economic optimism of the Year 2000 forecasters, in short, was flawed. They showed no awareness of the long K-waves of economic evolution, or the cyclical nature of socio-cultural dynamics. They did not factor in the entropic tendency of time.

Five years after the publication of *The Year 2000*, the Club of Rome introduced their world-famous 'limits to growth' paradigm. It was a far less optimistic perspective on the global future. It was modelled by an international team of sixteen academics in the Systems Dynamics Group of the Sloan School of Management in the Massachusetts Institute of Technology (MIT), led by Dennis Meadows.

Commissioned by the Club of Rome, an international group of scientists, businessmen and politicians, *Limits to Growth* introduced the benchmark of a sustainable future by analysing the 'long-term causes and consequences of growth in the world's population and material economy.' [336] A computer model (World3) was used to integrate data and theories about the concept of economic growth: 'With the model we can produce scenarios of world development that are internally consistent. In the first edition of *Limits to Growth* (LTG) we published and analyzed twelve scenarios from World3 that showed different possible patterns of world development over the two centuries from 1900 to 2100.' [337]

Meadows defines 'world' here as a huge and complex population-economy-environment system. The project team's major conclusion was that the world's ecological constraints, such as limits to natural resources and the absorption of pollution, would restrict global developments in the twenty-first century. The diversion of huge amounts of capital and manpower required to 'battle these constraints' would threaten growth.[338] This massive diversion of finance and labour, they argued, would lead to a decline in the average quality of life.

The authors measured humanity's ecological footprint [339] relative to the total carrying capacity of the earth's eco-systems: 'In our analysis we focused principally on the planet's physical limits, in the form of depletable natural resources and the finite capacity of the earth to absorb emissions from industry and agriculture. In every realistic scenario we found that these limits force an end to physical growth in World3 sometime during the twenty-first century. LTG placed the end of growth almost fifty years after the publication of the book.' [340] They warned that unsustainable growth would lead to collapse through overshoot: 'expansion in demands on the planet's sources...above levels that can be sustained'. [341]

The book offered an original environmentally-based perspective on possible global futures, rather than technology-based progressive socio-economic prognostications along the lines of H.G. Wells or the optimistic Year 2000 forecasts. The use of computer modelling to generate scenarios was also innovative at the time.

The authors urged policy-makers worldwide to plan ahead for the ecological crisis and invest in an orderly transition to a new kind of ecologically sound economic growth. The notion of future limits, central to the prognostic work of Malthus, Jevons and M. King Hubbert, was a cornerstone of this exceptional futurological work. But how accurate was their fifty year prediction of an end to high economic growth due to ecological constraints; the very opposite of the year 2000 predictions?

Meadows later outlined some data supporting their thesis that the world went into overshoot mode well within their chosen future time horizon: 'It now appears that the global per capita grain production peaked in the mid-1980s. The prospects for significant growth in the harvest of marine fish are gone. The costs of natural disasters are increasing, and there is growing intensity, even conflict, in efforts to allocate fresh water resources and fossil fuels among competing demands....Fifty-four nations, with twelve percent of the world population, experienced declines in per capita GDP for more than a decade during the period 1990 to 2001.' [342]

Added to this analysis, support for both the assumptions and the general accuracy of the World3 long-term predictions is provided by the following facts:

- The global economic recession, which began in 2008;
- The probable arrival of Peak Oil early in the first decade of this century, as predicted Hubbert in 1956;
- Rising levels of social unrest in several regions of the world due to increased food and energy prices;
- Socio-economic impacts of climate change.

The twenty-first century has, indeed, seen the large-scale economic slow-down originally forecast by the computer models of World3. Key projections or prognostications in *LTG* have been proven to have been accurate:

we can report that the highly aggregated scenarios of World3 still appear, after thirty years, to be surprisingly accurate. The world in the year 2000 had the same number of people (about 6 billion – up from the 3.9 billion in 1972) that we projected in the 1972 standard run of World3. Furthermore, that scenario showed growth in global food production (from 1.8 billion tons of grain equivalent per year in 1972 to 3 billion in 2000) that matches history quite well. Does this correspondence with history prove that our model was true? No, of course not. But it does indicate that World3 was not totally absurd; its assumptions and our conclusions still warrant consideration today. [343]

The *LTG* forecasts were based on assumptions from systems dynamics about the fundamental interdependence of systems (social, economic, environmental, etc). I support this approach as consistent with Biomatrix theory. In particular, they pinpointed three factors as underlying the 'dynamic patterns of behavior…of the global system', namely 'erodible limits, incessant pursuit of growth, and delays in society's responses to approaching limits', [344] correctly pointing out that physical limits of the planet cannot be wished away and need to be accounted for in any scientific prognostication of future growth.

Meadows asserts that current knowledge can be used to 'rule out a range of futures as unrealistic' as well as to present a range of alternative scenarios. [345] For forecasts to be accurate, they need to be based on correct assumptions as well as a complete set of data and information on the subject in question. They need to take into account all the interdependent variables which have an influence on that subject.

Subsequent history shows that the authors of *LTG* got their theory largely right. Their arguments have stood the test of time, and increased their relevance, whereas the optimism of the Year 2000 forecasts turned into a theoretical weakness.

However, it could be argued that the *LTG* scenarios underestimated the role of innovation in creating or changing the future. This is where pessimism can becloud analysis of the future as surely as optimism can. They assumed humanity would probably not find ways of overcoming and transcending the limits that were destined to confront them, that they would not invent new ways of creating wealth and pushing progress forward. Innovation was seen by Schumpeter, by contrast, as a driving force of economic development, resulting in widespread creative destruction, followed by growth of new technologies, sectors and even industries.

We have seen that history's cyclical nature, described in Chapter 11, renders redundant both optimistic and pessimistic approaches to human development. Both approaches suffer from imprecision and subjective projection. The forces of progress eternally thrust against opposing systemic inertia, until limits are reached to growth produced by current technologies and their production and distribution methods. They also come up against the ceilings of finite natural resources. This leads to a slowing of growth and possible social decline. The existence of both inertia and natural limits gives the lie to any blind optimism. But then innovations transcend the old limits and create new avenues to wealth creation and the next historic cycle of development starts up again. This ability of society to reinvent itself, displayed across the centuries, shows that pessimism is, ultimately, one-dimensional. Time's cyclical, evolutionary, long-range nature turns both optimism and pessimism into outdated approaches to the future. It is possible to be scientific in studying the behaviour of time and the behaviour of phenomena in time. Better than optimism and pessimism is a proactive, objective view of the time ahead of us.

CHAPTER 15
FUTURE OF THE FUTURE

Should a science of the future evolve as expected I would anticipate an escalating development of futurology, both in theory and in practice, over the next few decades.

Futures research has always been multi-disciplinary, drawing data and ideas from a range of sciences. The theory of foreknowledge proposed in this study has integrated principles from cosmology and space-time theory; social, historical and political science; population dynamics; energy resources and natural limits; economic science; urbanisation and transportation; and technological development.

Prognostic knowledge, or foreknowledge, is possible in these areas of scientific study when based on empirical induction and logical principles outlined in chapters 9 and 10. Multi-disciplinary foreknowledge would incorporate material from all of these areas to produce holistic 'big pictures' of the social future. An exciting era for social sciences in particular could open up with the institutionalised production of empirical foreknowledge. This would fuel a new anticipatory outlook on life.

Samet [346] has divided the field of futures study into three areas, each with distinct futurist schools from different sciences. Firstly, futures research, based on environmental and geosciences, on the one hand, and infrastructure and socio-technological systems on the other. Secondly, the category of futures studies covers the social, political, and economic sciences, as well as the human life, mind and information sciences. Finally, Samet's category of foresight includes business and management science. This is a useful classification. In addition, Futurology could be seen as the overarching study of the theory of foreknowledge and study of the future as a phase of evolutionary time. Samet's categorisation would show how foreknowledge could be positioned and applied within the different sciences.

Once futurology is established as a science, there would be nothing holding it back. Eventually, foreknowledge should transform knowledge itself, leading to an increase in the role of inter-disciplinary knowledge in general. There would be greater integration of knowledge across disciplines and across the world carried on the global 'brain' of the internet. There may even be a new synthesis between science and other non-scientific disciplines like philosophy and theology.

There will be a scramble for businesses, investors and consultancies to apply foreknowledge to yield a competitive edge. In addition, countries are likely to vie with one another in the race to develop capabilities for generating foreknowledge as they compete for influence and power in the evolving global order.

The scientific method will be at the forefront of this potential epistemological revolution. It remains a key tool for long-term human survival. The anti-scientific ideology of post-modernism is likely to recede into history, to be replaced by new modernism, the re-awakening of the idea of progress based on scientific knowledge and foreknowledge, contextualised within a post-industrial age of renewable energy.

Forward-looking societies will aim to achieve greater internal and external balance as they invest in their own futures and as they develop foreknowledge to combat systems inertia, entropic disorder and ecological collapse. Futuristic systems thinking will help societies and communities to develop stronger, more sustainable systems. Communities will strive to live in greater harmony with their surrounding environment in a great web of systems. The sciences of policy-making, decision-making and strategic planning will gain in efficiency, accuracy and influence.

In this process, society will draw ever closer to nature, our ultimate source of survival. We will witness humanity's largest return to the environment from whence it came since the end of the Agricultural Age. The Industrial Age will evolve into an Ecological Age in which there will be a strategic merger of the social and natural orders. In this trans-generational process, environmental science and ecology will continue to gain in value and influence. Likewise, physics will increase its importance to society by deepening our understanding of the universe and earth. Quantum physicist and futurist, Michio Kaku, applies the laws of physics to evaluate which technologies will shape the future of human civilisation.

As we peer into the increasingly visible far future, a new interest and investment in space travel will be ignited as we plan the first colonies on the moon and Mars. These will be mere baby steps in the ultimate plan of securing a base for human life beyond the solar system in our deep future. The aim would be to survive beyond the end of the sun's life and find other suns and planets which could energise the creation of inter-stellar civilisations. As a by-product of these futuristically inspired shifts of thinking towards the far future, it is possible that serious science fiction will gain a new impetus and importance in literature and in culture.

What will all this mean to humanity? The science of foreknowledge will enable human beings to become proactive and future-organised for the first time in history. We will gradually become adept at utilising the built-in evolutionary capacity of the brain to manipulate memories of the future. In turn, this will enhance sustainable lifestyles. Human destiny will be studied and understood as never before. We will feel more in control of our lives and societies, having learnt that it is not just space we must understand and conquer, but time as well. We will develop a new time-literate form of civilisation. If all goes according to plan, the number of socio-economic crises should gradually smooth out in the second half of this century, despite the threat of on-going global disorder identified in Chapter 13.

Additionally, it is likely that the chain of time between generations will be honoured once again as it was in ancient and medieval times. The knowledge of the future will spawn a renewed ethics of the future, where one generation will prepare the world for their grandchildren, great-grandchildren and even their great-great-grandchildren. Consequently the parochial and isolated post-modern nuclear family, which is bringing about significant depopulation to many advanced and emerging nations, will gradually be replaced by inter-generational families in an extended continuous two-hundred year present. This value shift will take the rest of the century.

Conversely, a repeat failure in the twenty-first century to embrace and create a science of futurology, mirroring what happened in the previous century, would prove fatal to the quest for an optimal human civilisation. It may even spell the beginning of the end of human evolution, making a regression into barbarism inevitable, especially given our built-in tectonic potential for international political disorder.

Short-termism in human thinking is the root of much evil in politics, economics, finance as well as in social and family relationships. In today's consumer society we have become immersed in what the great sociologist Pitirim Sorokin called 'temporalism'. The creed that 'tomorrow never comes' became an excuse for abandoning responsibilities towards the future. Foreknowledge and foresight are great antidotes to this toxic short-termism.

A deeper understanding of time should become a key to our future. Great physicists like Einstein and Hawking, more than anyone else, have illuminated the nature of time. Since humanity has explored most of planet earth and the moon, and has accumulated knowledge about the ends of the cosmos, this leaves time as our final frontier to explore and understand. More specifically, it points to the future as the next 'Promised Land' of knowledge.

Mathematician and cosmologist, Roger Penrose, described how cosmology matured from a 'speculative pursuit' into an 'exact science' following the discovery of cosmic microwave background (CMB) in the 1960s. CMB provided a wealth of evidence for the Big Bang theory of the origin of the universe. [347]

Futures studies today is still a speculative pursuit. Applying scientific principles of time in an epistemology of the future could be a catalyst for the discipline to undergo a similar theoretical maturation into a social science called futurology. [348]

Hawking recently alleged that philosophy is dead because 'it has not kept up with modern developments in science, particularly physics', leaving scientists, not philosophers, to be the torch-bearers of knowledge. [349] This is not the place to discuss this controversial but undeniably penetrating statement about the death of philosophy, but what is true is that scientific methods and disciplines remain fundamental to the advancement of knowledge about the world and society.

For this revolution in knowledge to take place, it is critical for futurology to become a scientific discipline. Foreknowledge at all times must satisfy the laws of logic, in particular the principle of *a priori* induction. It should be based on the influences of the laws of nature and social evolution, in particular, causation.

Referring back to the idea raised in the Foreword of this book likening future-watching to a form of pattern recognition, it is possible to consider causal influences as a filter through which we plot future patterns. Patterns of past evolution may be used to pre-construct future patterns, plotting the progress lines of any given entities while taking into account the impacts of causal influences arising from the laws of reality we have studied.

The three elementary shapes in Figure 15 represent any entity or social phenomenon. Progress lines run through their centres showing the trajectory of their evolution over time. The futurist looks at the patterns formed in past evolution. Then, armed with a causal map, as shown in Figure 13, he/she can identify how causal influences are likely to impact these evolutionary trajectories. Finally, future patterns are pre-constructed.

I recommend that the practice of social futurology, using preconstruction, should follow ten steps. In general, the futurologist should assume a quasi-deterministic future within the space-time continuum. In this continuum, the underlying laws of physics, especially those of thermodynamics, causation and chance, will act on the system in question in predictable ways. Society itself is located within space-time and is part of the evolutionary patterns formed by living, continuous time.

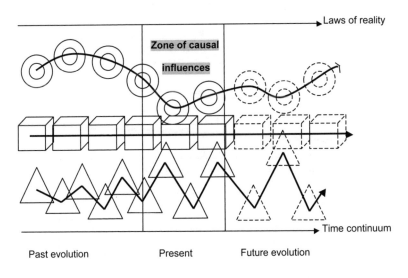

Figure 15. Preconstructing the future through pattern recognition

These ten steps for producing foreknowledge are illustrated in the diagram below.

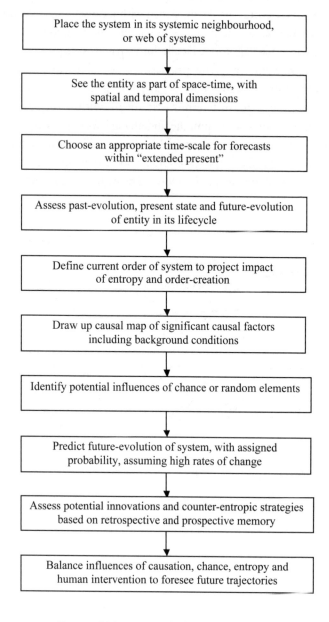

Figure 16. Ten-step model for foreknowledge

Futurologists will increase the scientific credibility of their work by incorporating as many of these ten steps as possible.

Step One
Place the system or entity in question, whether an organisation, a society or a social phenomenon, within its systemic neighbourhood, or web of systems.

Step Two
Conceive of the entity, or system, as part of the space-time continuum, with spatial and temporal dimensions, or coordinates, and subject to spatial and evolutionary influences.

Step Three
Choose an appropriate time-scale for forecasts or predictions as part of an 'extended two-hundred year present'.

Step Four
Assess the past-evolution and present state of the entity on its projected lifespan as the basis for building up knowledge of the future-evolution along its forecasted lifecycle.

Step Five
Define the current state of order of the system and its systemic neighbourhood in terms of a scale of high-order, medium-order or low-order, as a basis for projecting the effects of entropy and counter-entropic, order-creating strategies.

Step Six
Draw up a causal map (see Figure 13) of significant causal factors, including background conditions, in keeping with the principle in physics of antecedence. Included in causal factors should be fundamental influences like that of the role of energy in social development, and other important drivers identified in our story of the search for a science of the future.

Step Seven
Identify potential influences of chance, random or 'Black Swan' elements, bearing in mind long-term probabilities of such chance factors.

Step Eight

Outline provisional predicted outcomes of the future-evolution of the system in question within the chosen time-scale. Then assign a probability value to these outcomes ranging from certain to highly probable, on the scale of 0–1, excluding possibilities rated lower than 0.66. The probability will be based on expected influences of background causes, or conditions, on the system as well as direct causes. They will also be based on the assessment of the system's current state of order. A futurist will assume, other conditions being equal, increased entropy for ordered states and higher equilibrium for low order states when systems transformations take place. High rates of change should be assumed in all cases, too, given the nature of cosmological time.

Step Nine

Assess the potential role of psychological time, and memories, both retrospective and prospective, on the entity in the chosen time-scale; construct possible scenarios of human interventions in the system's neighbourhood, especially counter-entropic strategies. This step could lead to a refinement of the provisional predicted outcomes in Step Eight.

Step Ten

Conduct a final check of the revised predicted outcomes by balancing anticipated influences of causation, chance, entropy and the creative power of human intervention and innovations to produce forecasted future trajectories towards an evolving future.

Alongside renewable energy, knowledge is the most important renewable resource for keeping humanity's progress on track in the twenty-first century and beyond.

Throughout this book, the story of the search for a scientific approach to the future has been told. This can be represented in a synoptic timeline (Figure 17).

This timeline shows how knowledge has evolved to a point where we have marshalled the key concepts needed for a discipline of futurology. The core of this theoretical framework is the physics of time. Underpinning the new science of foreknowledge should be a universal respect for time and the future.

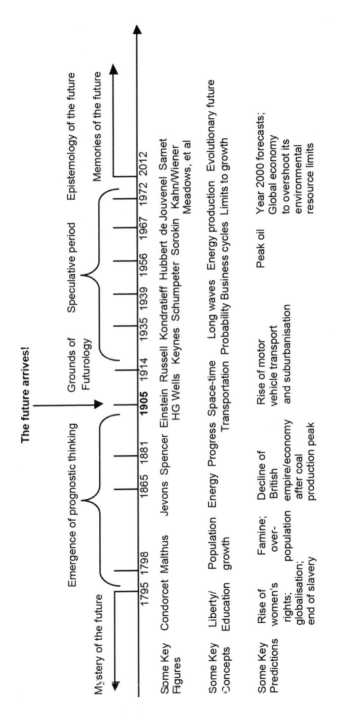

Figure 17. Concise timeline in evolution of futurology

In space-time, time is spatialised as a dimension of real experience, losing, in the process, some of its mystery. The future is now more accessible to conceptual understanding. Time is an intimate part of all experience, an active, physical shaper of human destiny and social development.

Space-time is continuously evolving towards the future. This is the inherent direction of time, the cosmic medium of evolutionary change. The future is of special importance to science and to society. The principle of antecedence in physics shows that all phenomena emerge from other prior states and phenomena. Time itself emerges continuously from past time into future time across the transitional swing bridge of the present.

If we can break through the knowledge barrier between current knowledge and foreknowledge, using logical methods, it will enable us to take possession of the future.

CHAPTER 16
INVASION OF THE FUTURE

In 2012, I was privileged to meet Dr Buzz Aldrin at a conference my organisation had arranged in San Antonio, Texas, where he was featured as a motivational speaker. As the second of only twelve astronauts ever to walk on the surface of another celestial body, he has unique credentials. He was with Neil Armstrong for the historic Apollo 11 moon landing, one of the bravest and most successful human projects of all time.

I confess to being awestruck when I met this long-time hero and living legend. However, his warmth and charm quickly won over the audience and relaxed me. One part in his stirring keynote address stood out for me. When President Kennedy had committed America to the ambitious dream of landing men on the moon and returning them safely to earth, the country did not possess all the necessary knowledge and technology required for this dangerous mission. Yet, against the odds, exerting collective willpower in a team numbering about 400,000 individuals in total, the lofty goal was successfully accomplished (only just, it should be noted) within the stipulated time frame. It was then that Buzz asked the audience a simple, but daunting, question: what is the next impossible dream?

Sitting in the audience after having opened the conference, I instantly thought I knew the answer. I was convinced there and then that the next impossible dream for humanity was not going to Mars. The next mission would be an invasion of the future. And we will need to use the same method used to take Apollo 11 to Tranquillity Base, namely the theory and application of science. Science is the spaceship in which we can travel into the future.

It is common practice in physics to refer to the arrow of time. This metaphor conveys the idea that time moves in one direction only: forwards. This concept is quite correct but there is a problem with the metaphor itself. Its connotation is that time is like an object or thing, external to experience. But time is more like a living process. It is a physical dimension in space-time which surrounds us. In time we live, move and have our being. We are inside both time and space. Yet time itself, like space, is a moving vehicle. And it is taking us in the direction in which it it programmed to go, that is, the future. We are travelling through a wondrous 4D world which itself is moving very fast.

The space-time continuum is being continuously stretched by the accelerating expansion of the universe in what Hawking called cosmological time.[350] The more distant a galaxy is from earth, the faster it is speeding away: 'galaxies that are 100 million light-years from us are moving away at about 5.5 million miles per hour, those at 200 million light-years are moving away twice as fast…'.[351] These incredible speeds are virtually inconceivable. No wonder everything is in motion, all of the time; no wonder our journey through time is a bumpy, yet exhilarating, ride, yielding constant change and even turbulence. All things evolve within this high-speed cosmological time in our highly mobile universe.

Yet if things were not in motion, if space and time were not in motion, there would be no life. Were it not for motion, and the principles of motion, such as the laws of motion and the workings of gravity, Newton went on to argue, 'the bodies of the earth, planets, comets, sun and all things in them, would grow cold and freeze, and become inactive masses; and all putrefaction, generation, vegetation, and life would cease, and the planets and comets would not remain in their orbits.'[352]

The story of time shows us that it is irreversible, moving with an urgency into the future as if the Big Bang stamped a destiny onto existence at Time Zero. The ship of time never, ever loses its direction. What makes sense in such a world is to be aligned to it, orientated towards the future.

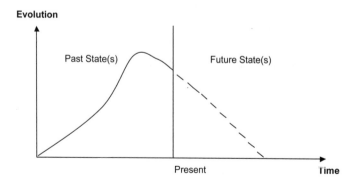

Figure 18. Plotting future-evolution

What counts for individuals, organisations and societies is to be evolving towards something better. History shows this in the forms of social progress we have witnessed. That's the core message of the future. Time has written a letter to humanity in the language of science urging us to *evolve, advance!* [353] And futurology can accelerate humanity's progress through the application of foreknowledge. The ten-step model in Figure 16 indicates how to produce such foreknowledge by which the future-evolution of phenomena may be plotted on their lifespan trajectory, yielding a probable timeline for their predicted future state.

The Copernican or Gott principle, discussed in Chapter 12, may be employed to assist in determining the most likely time-frames for the duration of a lifespan. The time-spans developed by Samet for the long-range social future will also prove useful, as will the long economic K-waves, and Schumpeter's shorter business cycles, for assessing the future duration of economic phenomena.

Predictive knowledge is like squeezing the future out of a tube in which all the possible influences of causation, and, to a lesser extent, those from chance variables, have been packed. It is like filtering one narrow future out of a funnel of possibilities. In the space-time continuum, there can only be a single future for all.

We can steer the spaceship of time, in which we are all passengers, using scientific knowledge and principles. The ten-step futurological model in Figure 16 is based on applying the concepts of physics to the operations of phenomena in society – what forces and influences will bring about which new phenomena or changes to existing entities? What effects of entropy will there be? What forces of inertia are there in the systems in question? What are the most powerful causes? What background factors will play a role in shaping the future?

We have a greater understanding of the behaviour of social phenomena in and through time than ever before. We have mapped out universal lifecycles in nature and society. They are not mysteries. They are knowable and predictable.

Future knowledge is based on understanding the nature of time. Future states will range from high order to high disorder. Increasing disorder over time will characterise a default future in which no level of future organisation is imposed on the system, or subject, in question.

What counts is how time is used to organise for the future. Organising for the future aims at generating momentum to overcome inertia. Inertia preserves the current state and is passive in nature. The longer inertia prevails the more pronounced the effects of entropy (or dissolution of structure in its general, non-technical sense) will become. The proactive frame of mind aims to generate momentum and to create order out of disorder. Momentum is targeted, or directed, use of energy to create order out of naturally spreading chaos.

It is possible that this struggle between applying energy to create order and the change and diffusion of structure over time is only a surface manifestation of a deeper conflict. In Hawking's three-fold approach to time, there is psychological, or what could be called human, time, as well as cosmological and entropic time, which together make up the concept of cosmic time, or the time of the universe. There is a creative tension between human time and cosmic time. It is possible the fluctuations we have observed in social dynamics in Chapter 11 are, at heart, driven by the changing relationship, or interaction, between human time and cosmic time. We want to create states of high order but time so often brings diffusion, disintegrating structure and lower order. The latter brings change and disorder while humanity seeks to impose order.

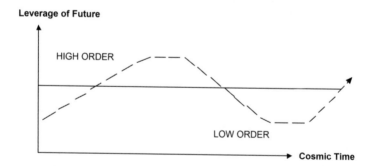

Figure 19. Creative tension of time

Throughout history, there has been a battle between the forces of innovation and growth opposed to inertia, stagnation, disorder and decline. We also see in this struggle the possibility of shifting trajectories of time between the poles of a default future as opposed to a more ordered future, one closer to a structured outcome called destiny.

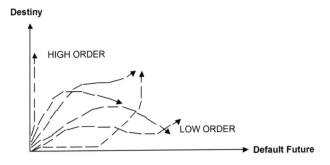

Figure 20. Shifting short-term trajectories of time

In Figure 20, destiny is the creation of states of high order. The logic of time is its purpose, its direction. Put another way, it is the leverage exerted by reasonable human use of time over cosmic time and its effects. Time, like space, is flexible as space-time stretches across the universe. Therefore, it is likely that time, like space, can be shaped and calibrated by human enterprise. Archimedes claimed that with one lever he could move the world. Foreknowledge is the lever that will move time. Certainly it is possible to leverage time, to shift time trajectories towards the pole of destiny away from a default future.

What held back the development of true foreknowledge in the twentieth century, despite the enormous potential for effective long-term social foresight demonstrated by prognostic thinkers from Condorcet to H.G. Wells, was a failure to define the future as a form of time. For centuries, there has been a myth of the impenetrable mystery of the future. Thanks to physics, this ancient mystery has been illuminated. A theoretical door has been opened to develop prognostic knowledge to better understand human destiny.

The discovery of the space-time continuum by Einstein unlocked the secrets of time. Einstein wanted us to measure all four dimensions of experience, the three spatial coordinates plus the time dimension. Instead of revering the mystery of time, we can now respect the reality of time.

The discipline of physics has been at the cutting edge of human knowledge ever since Einstein broke through to a new understanding of how the world really works. Furthermore, the physics of time provides futurology with an ontology. The future now has an epistemology. The future of the future looks very promising.

The human brain is certainly ready for this new era of knowing our future. It is already wired to develop what Russell called memory of the future. The mind is geared up to use memory to anticipate future events, creating intuitive scenarios in order to be mentally prepared for all eventualities. This ability has been called mental time travel, described by some psychologists as our best weapon in human adaptation. In *Physics of the Future* Kaku defines the three basic acts of human consciousness as sensing the environment, self-awareness and planning for the future. Knowing our future does not create it, however, it merely anticipates it: 'prevision would not create the future any more than memory creates the past'. [354]

The gift of futurology is not just foresight or foreknowledge, however valuable and useful prognostic knowledge can be. It is the inspiration to adopt a proactive mind-set. A habit of being anticipatory in outlook, in turn, will bring greater boldness and decisiveness in getting things done. [355]

Physics shows us that the world is rushing towards the future at high speed. Through the windscreen of time we can see that visibility has improved ahead of us. Finally, we can see the shape of tomorrow coming to meet us.

APPENDIX 1
THE TEN GREATEST PREDICTIONS OF ALL TIME

It is mid-September, 1930, in Germany. Significant electoral gains have seen the Nazi Party become the country's second biggest party in terms of the number of seats in Parliament. Hitler believes his moment has come, proclaiming boldly that the Nazis will win the next election and that their rise to the pinnacle of power is now inevitable and unstoppable.

Fast forward eighteen years to 14 May 1948. Outside Tel Aviv Museum in Palestine, the Jewish People's Council approves a proclamation declaring the establishment of the new State of Israel. Meanwhile, Hitler's Thousand-Year Reich has come crashing down a full 985 years too early after orchestrating the worst crime in human history.

It is during this cataclysmic period of modern history between 1930 and 1948 that we encounter two of the best predictions of all time. The first is Winston Churchill's warning to the British parliament in 1933 that a second major European war would take place in the foreseeable future as a result of German rearmament and deep-seated grievances. The second is the fulfilment of an ancient prophecy about the founding of a homeland for the Jews after centuries of exile and statelessness.

I will analyse both forecasts, along with eight other stunning examples of social foresight, but first we need to decide how to measure the degree of success of a prediction. This will enable us to rank these ten predictions in order of merit. It is proposed that prescience, defined generally as knowing about something before it happens, is produced by far-sightedness, the ability to look ahead in time, combined with a sense of the scale, magnitude or importance of the subject matter to society. In addition, the logic or method informing the prediction should be sound. By these three criteria, predictions which look far ahead, give insight into momentous, world-changing events and employ strong theoretical logic could be considered great.

In April 1933, Churchill uttered these prescient words in parliament: 'as surely as Germany acquires full military equality with her neighbours while her own grievances are still unaddressed and while she is in the temper which we have unhappily seen, so surely shall we see ourselves within a measurable distance of the renewal of general European war'.[356] Six years later, on 1 September 1939, Germany invaded Poland. It is thought some 60 million people died in the war that followed. Although Churchill's prediction was not *far*-sighted time-wise, it was certainly momentous on a historical scale. His logic was that Germany's humiliation in the first war provided a deep-seated motive for its resurgence and eventual aggression.

While in exile in ancient Babylon, the major Hebrew prophet Ezekiel, in his public career from 593–571 BC, described detailed visions of the future national restoration of the then stateless Israelites. Some of these visions can apply to the establishment of a modern state of Israel in 1948, 1,878 years after the destruction by the Romans of the second temple in Jerusalem in AD 70. We know that the founding of modern Israel occurred only a few short years after the harrowing events of the Holocaust. Significantly, Ezekiel referred to the founding of a new country of Israel after an 'outpouring of wrath/fury' [20:34]. The Hebrew word for 'fury' used in this particular verse is *chêmâh*, which connoted fever resulting from being poisoned. The word could have signified poisonous rage, an apt description of the murderous racial hatred which motivated Hitler's so-called Final Solution. If we join together various verses from Ezekiel's prophecies of national restoration, we can get a sense of how he foresaw this event happening in a way which locates the fulfilment of the historical vision in modern Israel, rather than in ancient Palestine at the time of the second temple: 'I will bring you from the nations and gather you from the countries where you have been scattered – with a mighty hand and an outstretched hand and with outpoured wrath [20:44]….You will live in the land I gave your forefathers [36:28]….This is where I will live among the Israelites forever [43:7].' The word 'forever' in the last verse denotes permanence which is why it cannot refer to Israel's second temple which lasted from 516 BC to AD 70. The time period from the start of Ezekiel's prophetic ministry in 593 to the founding of Israel in1948 is simply enormous: just under two and a half millennia.

Although on a smaller time scale, another remarkable and far-sighted prediction was made by an Enlightenment thinker at the time of the French Revolution about the future rise of equal political rights for women, just under a century before this came to pass in the real world. We are talking about a man who deserves to be seen as the grandfather of a modern study of the future.

Although he cannot be described as a futurist, the Marquis de Condorcet (1743–1794), was certainly a prognostic thinker. He anticipated the increase of political equality in a new era in which scientific knowledge, allied to liberty, was destined to play a decisive role in society. A French mathematician, philosopher and political scientist, Condorcet concluded his study of the history of humanity's intellectual and moral development with a chapter on the future progress of mankind as he foresaw it. In this penetrating look into the far future, he wrote, with unconcealed passion: 'Among those causes of human improvement that are of the most importance to the general welfare, must be included, the total annihilation of the prejudices which have established between the sexes an inequality of rights, fatal even to the party which it favours….And here we may observe, how much the abolition of the usages authorised by this prejudice, and of the laws it has dictated, would tend to augment the happiness of families…'.

British suffragette Mary Wollstonecraft published *A Vindication of the Rights of Women* in 1792, but the first country to grant women suffrage in national elections was New Zealand in 1893, just under a century after the posthumous publication of Condorcet's treatise on progress.

In addition to predicting the rise of women's rights several decades before it happened, Condorcet also foresaw the coming of an extensive economic globalisation process: 'the moment knowledge shall have arrived at a certain pitch in a great number of nations at once, the moment it shall have penetrated the whole mass of a great people, [a] whole language shall have become universal, and the whole commercial intercourse shall embrace the whole extent of the globe'. Again, these words, perhaps history's first definition of globalisation, are deeply foresightful. I have allocated this French thinker first and third positions on the league table of great predictions (at the end of this appendix).

Thomas Malthus (1766–1834), a clergyman and economist, wrote *An Essay on the Principle of Population* in 1798 just a few years after Condorcet died. Malthus argued that population growth in the long-run tended to outrun a country's means of subsistence, especially its food production rate. He predicted that the modern era would experience huge famines due to over-population. It has proved true that starvation and malnutrition have haunted the modern era amidst all the wonderful signs of progress, including the Great Irish Famine of 1846–1851, the Ethiopian famine of 1888–1891, the Soviet famine of 1931–1933, the Great Chinese Famine of 1959–1961, as well as famines in Biafra in the late 1960s, Ethiopia in 1984–5 and North Korea in the 1990s, to mention only a few.

The nineteenth century witnessed further attempts at long-range social forecasts. The most prognostic was *The Coal Question* by British economist and logician W. Stanley Jevons. This 1865 treatise forecast the depletion of the country's coal mines during the ensuing one hundred years. Jevons correctly identified the crucial role of industrial energy in determining a nation's socio-economic future. This book is one of the best works of factual foresight ever written.

Jevons was concerned about two things: namely, the loss of Britain's economic supremacy due to the shrinking of its coal resources and the long-term social decline this would cause. Just over ninety years after the publication of *The Coal Question*, US geophysicist M. King Hubbert confirmed that the production pattern for world coal production had, as anticipated by Jevons, peaked, leading to sharp declines in the post-peak period. Hubbert illustrated the steep decline in production of coal after 1925, confirming the general accuracy of Jevons' main thesis regarding Britain's anticipated 'Peak Coal'.

Hubbert himself produced, in my view, the twentieth century's greatest predictions. In a paper entitled 'Nuclear Energy and the Fossil Fuels' presented to the American Petroleum Institute in San Antonio, Texas, in March 1956, Hubbert, then employed by Shell, correctly predicted that US oil production would peak within twenty years by the early 1970s. He also forecast that global oil production would peak at the turn of the century. Due to the accuracy of his prognostications, he has become known as the father of the theory of Peak Oil. This phenomenon has far-reaching worldwide implications for our own times. It could become the biggest change in industrial history, a turning-point in the evolution of human society.

But Hubbert was a geophysicist, not a futurist. The greatest pioneer of the systematic study of the future was H.G. Wells, science fiction writer and the world's first real futurist. In 1901 Wells wrote *Anticipations*, the earliest attempt at a scientific study of the long-range social future. The

book's stated aim was to outline 'a rough sketch of the coming time...
[an] anticipatory balance-sheet'. Wells set out to construct a 'picture of
a human community somewhere towards the year 2000'. *Anticipations*
presented a one-hundred year vision of society as the twentieth century
was beginning.

The point of departure for Wells' vision of the future was that
transportation systems constitute the most critical catalyst for broad social
development: 'upon transport, upon locomotion, may also hang the most
momentous issues of politics and war'. He regarded the steam engine, for
example, as the dominant transport technology of the nineteenth century
in Britain. He explained that cities and towns had developed around key
transport, or transit nodes, creating a 'railway world'. Based on this logic,
he predicted that new motorised vehicles, namely trucks carrying goods,
motor omnibuses transporting people *en masse* and privately owned motor
vehicles, would compete with the railways and create new transportation
systems. There would be widespread development of roads specifically for
motor vehicle use. Time has proved his forecasts of a transport revolution
to have been accurate. The twentieth century did turn out to be dominated
by suburban and urban development built around motor vehicles and the
road system which transported them. We still live today in the motorised
world predicted by Wells in *Anticipations*. That fact demonstrates how
momentous his 1901 forecasts really were (although he also got a lot of
forecasts wrong in the book due to faulty theorising).

Finally, I regard J. Richard Gott's forecast about the fall of the Berlin
Wall as a breakthrough prediction because it was based on the precise use
of mathematical probabilities. In 1969 Gott, an American astrophysicist,
visited this menacing wall and wondered how long it would remain in
place.

His scientific training told him that Copernicus had shown
that earth did not occupy a special position in the solar system. It was
logical to extend this argument, he thought, to the idea that no location
anywhere in space or in time is ever special. 'If there was nothing special
about the location of my visit in time, there was a fifty percent chance
that I was observing the wall sometime during the middle two quarters
of its existence....So standing at the wall in 1969, I predicted...that there
was a fifty percent chance that the future longevity of the wall would be
between two and two-third years and twenty-four years....When the wall

came down in 1989, after twenty years, in agreement with my original prediction, I decided that I should write this up.'

Gott's principle is that we observe things at random, i.e. non-special, times so that there is always a fifty percent chance that we are doing so in the middle of their lifespan. You just have to find out their start date, as Gott did when he visited that oppressive symbol of the Cold War. He developed a smart and unique way of estimating the future duration of entities, from buildings to organisations, from species to societies.

Evaluating these ten predictions according to how far-sighted, socially significant and theoretically logical they turned out to be, we arrive at the following rankings and conclusions, by allocating 5 points for 'very high' down to 1 point for 'low' for each of our three criteria of successful predictions.

In terms of social predictions, the honour of producing the best ever forecasts must go to the Frenchman Condorcet for accurately foreseeing the rise of both equal women's rights and the global economy, two world-changing developments he anticipated many decades ahead of their time. Another European forecast in the table of top ten predictions is the work of the Club of Rome for understanding back in 1972 that environmental constraints would ultimately put the brakes on global economic growth and force the world to look more closely at the systems concept of sustainability.

The table also features four world-class British forecasts, namely the ways motorisation would change the nature of society throughout the twentieth century (H.G. Wells in 1901), the long-range forecast of the loss of Britain's economic supremacy due to decline in its coal reserves (Jevons in 1865), the rise of famines in the modern era caused by overpopulation (Malthus in 1798) and the coming of World War Two (Churchill in 1933).

Two American thinkers have made important contributions to the world's heritage of great predictions. M. King Hubbert is the father of Peak Oil, one of the most important theories of our time. And the method J. Richard Gott used to predict the fall of the Berlin Wall twenty years before it happened holds much promise for developing knowledge of the future lifespans of a wide range of entities.

Together, these ten historical predictions decisively show the way forward for the human production of social foresight.

Table 4 Top ten predictions of all time

Forecaster	Prediction	Date of prediction	Date when prediction was fulfilled	Far-sighted	Momentous	Logic	Rank
Marquis de Condorcet	Rise of equal rights for women	1795	From 1893	Very high (5)	Very high (5)	High (4)	1st (14)
M. King Hubbert	Peak Oil for USA and world	1956	1970 and 2000 respectively	High (4)	High (4)	Very high (5)	2nd (13)
Marquis de Condorcet	Rise of economic globalisa-tion	1795	From Bretton Woods July 1944	Very high (5)	High (4)	High (4)	3rd (13)
Club of Rome think-tank led by Dennis L. Meadows	Slowing down of global economic growth due to ecological and environmental constraints with an end to all high growth by 2022	1972	From the 2008 credit crisis and subsequent euro zone crisis onwards	High (4)	High (4)	Very High (5)	4th (13)
H.G. Wells	Motorisation of society in twentieth century	1901	From debut of Ford's Model T in 1908	Moderate (2)	Very high (5)	Very high (5)	5th (12)

W. Stanley Jevons	Decline of British global supremacy due to depletion of coal resources	1865	From the steep decline in production of coal after 1925	High (4)	Moderate to high (3)	Very high (5)	6th (12)
Ezekiel	National restoration of Israel after lengthy exile and following a time of 'outpoured wrath'	593–571 BC	1948	Very high (5)	High (4)	Moderate (2)	7th (11)
Thomas Malthus	Rise of famine due to over-population in modern era	1798	From Great Irish Famine of 1846–1851 to famine in North Korea in 1990s	High (4)	High (4)	Moderate to high (3)	8th (11)
Winston Churchill	Outbreak of Second World War due to German rearmament	1933	1939	Moderate (2)	High (4)	High (4)	9th (10)
J. Richard Gott	Fall of the Berlin Wall	1969	1989	Moderate to high (3)	Moderate (2)	Very high (5)	10th (10)

APPENDIX 2
EVIDENCE SUPPORTING THE THEORY OF RELATIVITY

Einstein's conception of space-time, part of special relativity, is the key to understanding both time and the future. This theory is highly regarded in contemporary physics as the prevailing model for explaining how the macroscopic world works. It is supported by a wealth of experimental evidence.

The most sensational evidence for the theory was gleaned during the solar eclipse of 1919. The proof turned Einstein into an overnight global celebrity. But he wrote matter-of-factly of this evidence: 'We are indebted to the [British] Royal Society and to the Royal Astronomical Society.... Undaunted by the [first world] war...these societies equipped two expeditions – to Sobral [Brazil] and to the island of Principe [West Africa] – and sent several of Britain's most celebrated astronomers...in order to obtain photographs of the solar eclipse of 29th May, 1919....The results of the measurements confirmed the theory [of relativity] in a thoroughly satisfactory manner.' [357]

In his paper 'The Foundation of the Generalised Theory of Relativity', published in 1916 in *Annalen der Physik*, Einstein predicted that 'a ray of light just grazing the sun would suffer a bending of 1.7, whereas one coming by Jupiter would have a deviation of about .02'. [358] Experiments later proved him accurate in his predictions.

The increasingly popular GPS systems people use in their cars today could not function accurately without taking into account the effects of relativity: 'The satellite navigation system in your car, for example, is designed to account for the fact that time ticks at a different rate on the orbiting satellites than it does on the ground.... The GPS satellite system is ubiquitous...and its successful functioning depends on the accuracy of Einstein's theories'. [359]

The reason for these different rates of time is that gravity is weaker for clocks on satellites so these clocks speed up at a rate of 45 microseconds each day. The satellites move at high speeds and we know Einstein proved that clocks tick at a slower rate at higher speeds. If these two opposite effects are added, there is a net acceleration of 38 microseconds per day. Any failure to factor in these dilating and contracting effects on time would lead to a breakdown of GPS systems. This is a practical and easily understood vindication of Einstein's theory.

In 1962, the prediction that time runs at a slower rate near a massive body, such as our earth, was tested using a water tower. The experiment once again confirmed the effects of relativity: 'This prediction was tested in 1962, using a pair of very accurate clocks mounted at the top and bottom of a water tower. The clock at the bottom, which was nearer the earth, was found to run slower, in exact agreement with general relativity.' [360]

Then in 1971, more striking evidence supporting Einstein's theory was gathered. Hawking described this experiment: 'imagine a reference clock at rest at the centre of the earth, another clock on the earth's surface, and a third clock aboard a plane flying either with or against the direction of the earth's rotation. With reference to the clock at the earth's centre, the clock aboard the plane moving eastwards – in the direction of the earth's rotation – is moving faster than the clock on the earth's surface, and so it should run slower. Similarly, with reference to the clock at the earth's centre, the clock aboard the plane flying westward – against the earth's rotation – is moving slower than the surface clock, which means that clock should run faster than the clock on the surface. And that is exactly what was observed when, in an experiment performed in October 1971, a very accurate atomic clock was flown around the world.' [361]

Then there was the so-called muon test. Muons are particles that live for the grand time of 2.2 microseconds when at rest. Late in the 1990s, scientists at the Alternating Gradient Synchroton (AGS) on Long Island, NY, built a machine shooting beams of muons around a ring at the speed of 99.94% of the speed of light: 'If muons live for only 2.2 microseconds when they are speeding around the ring, then they would manage only fifteen laps of the ring before they died. In reality, they managed more like 400 laps, which means their lifetime is extended by a factor of twenty-nine to just over sixty microseconds'. [362] These amazing particles extended their lives by travelling fast, thus slowing down their rate of time.

Experimental evidence for Einstein's relativity model has continued to pour in.

For example, binary pulsar experiments have reinforced the truths of relativity: 'The orbit of the binary pulsar spins itself up exactly in accordance with the theory of general relativity and the accompanying idea that gravitational radiation leads to orbital decay. The binary pulsar thus allows us to measure the predictions of general relativity extremely accurately. Joe Taylor and Russell Hulse discovered this system in 1974 and performed careful timing measurements over the next two decades. Their results are in stunning agreement with the predictions of general relativity…'. [363]

Then in 2007 there was a new time-dilation experiment: 'a team of scientists led by Gerald Gwinner of the University of Manitoba confirmed the time-dilation effect to one part in 10 million. Gwinner and his colleagues used an accelerator in Germany to whip lithium ions through a circular tube at six percent of the speed of light. They then used a laser to stimulate the ions, forcing them to give off radiation…the radiation…can act as a clock….At the high speeds involved, the ticks slowed down…the frequency shift was just that predicted by special relativity'. [364]

In addition to all the observational support for Einstein's view of the world, gathered between 1919 and 2007, there is the amazing fact that the Standard Model of Particle Physics, the so-called master equation of physics, is entirely based on relativity: 'the whole structure rests firmly on Einstein's special theory of relativity'. [365] Physicist Brian Cox explains: 'the idea of spacetime leads naturally to e = mc2 ….this simple equation and the physics it represents has become a foundation stone of…modern theories of nature and the industrial world'. [366]

APPENDIX 3
WHY THE UNCERTAINTY PRINCIPLE IS OVERRATED AND MISCONSTRUED

One of the five factors which led to a failure to develop a science of the future in the twentieth century was the powerful intellectual influence of post-modernism. This cultural movement tried to deconstruct the whole paradigm of modern Western civilisation, including the cardinal role of science and rationality in acquiring knowledge, as well as its traditional value systems derived from philosophy, ethics, economics and religion as shaping forces of society. Pessimistic post-modernism infected the discipline of futures studies, as well as most other social sciences.

In some ways, this was based on a misconception that Einstein's relativity meant that the world now had no absolutes, not in religion, not in ethics, not in philosophy, not in culture and not in knowledge. Yet Einstein originally wanted to call his theory the Invariant Theory. It was based on the constancy of the speed of light, which is absolute.

But post-modernism also gained philosophical momentum from the uncertainty principle, formulated by Werner Heisenberg in 1926. It seemed to provide a theoretical licence to deconstruct reason even more. Hawking explains the uncertainty principle: 'In order to predict the future position and velocity of a particle, one has to be able to measure its present position and velocity accurately…[but] the more accurately you try to measure the position of the particle, the less accurately you can measure its speed, and vice versa.…The uncertainty principle signaled an end to Laplace's dream of a theory of science, a model of the universe that would be completely deterministic.…In general, quantum mechanics does not predict a single definite result for an observation. Instead, it predicts a number of different possible outcomes.…Quantum mechanics therefore introduces an unavoidable element of unpredictability or randomness into science.' [367]

There *is* a very high degree of unpredictability at the quantum level. Probabilities in quantum theory reflect a 'fundamental randomness in nature' with particles appearing to take every possible path from the start point to the end point simultaneously! [368]

But then we are also entitled to ask the sacrilegious question, so what? That is because quantum mechanics deals with phenomena on 'extremely small scales, such as a millionth of a millionth of an inch'. [369]

The reason why this uncertainty principle, and the randomness it implies, is not as influential at the level of human life is that there are ontological thresholds at the levels of planetary, macroscopic and microscopic existence, each with their own distinctive principles and laws. These thresholds can be represented in a Venn diagram.

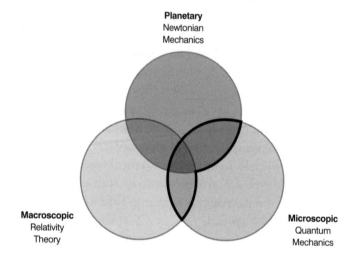

Figure 21. Three domains of physics with ontological thresholds

Figure 21 shows ontological thresholds between the quantum level, the 'life-size' level of everyday existence and the cosmic level of planets and galaxies: 'The entities at the macroscopic level must have at least some relative autonomy in their modes of being, in the sense that these modes cannot be predicted perfectly in the specific lower level (or levels) in question.' [370] For example, motion becomes much more violent the deeper physics goes into the atomic level and below. [371]

While the Venn diagram in Figure 21 indicates areas of overlap between the domains, [372] there are also thresholds, marked by bold black lines, beyond which any overlapping forces are too weak to produce significant effects. Atoms, for example, may be too small to have an appreciable effect on the whole, large-scale entities of which they are tiny parts. Bohm speaks of the 'insensitivity of the overall large-scale behaviour to precisely what the individual molecules are doing'. [313] Kaku states that the rules governing atoms are different from the rules governing galaxies. [314]

Bohm declares that the macroscopic level possesses 'relatively autonomous qualities' which satisfy 'relatively autonomous relations' which, in turn, enable 'a set of macroscopic causal laws'. [315] For each level of existence, as depicted in Figure 21, from the macroscopic to the microscopic and sub-atomic, 'we find the typical relative autonomy of behaviour and the existence of sets of qualities, laws and relationships which are characteristic of the level in question'. [316] It is therefore a moot point whether it makes sense to apply the uncertainty principle, operational at the atomic and sub-atomic levels of existence, at the macroscopic level. [317]

Futurology, and the social sciences in general, focus on the domain of macroscopic reality. Here the theory of relativity governs the physical understanding of the world, in which there is an inherent fabric of laws, including causation and chance and the inter-relationship between them: 'a macroscopic level possessing a set of relatively autonomous qualities and satisfying a set of relatively autonomous relations which effectively constitute a set of macroscopic causal laws'. [318]

The ontological autonomy for different levels of existence in physics paves the way for futurology to focus on the application of causal laws, and chance, at this macroscopic level, without undue attention being paid to the principles of quantum mechanics. At this level, it is the theory of relativity which is the governing theory of physics: 'Einstein's general theory of relativity seems to govern the large-scale structure of the universe.' [319] Hawking reinforces the principle of autonomy between these ontological levels: 'For practical calculations involving the everyday world, we can continue to use classical theories.' [320]

Largely as a result of the ontological thresholds shown in Figure 21, quantum mechanics does not undermine the essential lawfulness of nature as represented by classical physics: 'Quantum physics might seem to undermine the idea that nature is governed by laws, but that is not the case...it leads us to accept a new form of determinism: given the state of a system at some time, the laws of nature determine probabilities of various futures and pasts rather than determining the future and past with certainty…it is important to realise that probabilities in quantum physics are not like probabilities in Newtonian physics, or in everyday life.' [381]

In short, quantum mechanics does not apply at the level of macroscopic observed reality which is the domain of the social sciences: 'for most practical purposes quantum theory does not hold much relevance for the study of large-scale structure of the universe because quantum theory applies to the description of nature on microscopic scales'. [382]

Perhaps the last word on this matter belongs to Hawking: 'Quantum physics provides a framework for understanding how nature operates on atomic and subatomic scales…though the components of everyday objects obey quantum physics, Newton's laws form an effective theory that describes very accurately how the composite structures that form our everyday world behave…the larger the object the less apparent and robust are the quantum effects.' [383]

Futurology, the social sciences, and human culture in general, need not fear, nor exaggerate the importance of, the uncertainty principle – or the tiniest of particles whose behaviour it describes.

END NOTES

Chapter 1. The Lens of Time

1 Bell, *Foundations of Futures Studies – Human Science for a New Era*, Vol 1 (2003) 140.

2 Graf, P & Grondin, S, et al., *Timing the Future – The case for a time-based prospective memory* (2006) 8.

3 Suddendorf, T., Addis, D.R., & Corballis, M.C., 'Mental time travel and the shaping of the human mind' (2009) *Philosophical Transactions of the Royal Society* 1317–1324.

Chapter 2. Pioneering a Science of the Future

4 Condorcet, *Outlines of an historical view of the progress of the human mind* (1795) 355–6.

5 Ibid. 14–15.

6 Ibid. 4.

7 Condorcet asserted that 'nature has indissolubly united the advancement of knowledge with the progress of liberty, virtue and respect for the natural rights of man'. At the core of this process is the way in which the various sciences extend knowledge: 'The progress of the sciences secures the progress of the art of instruction, which again accelerates in its turn that of the sciences; and this reciprocal influence, the action of which is incessantly increased, must be ranked in the number of the most prolific and powerful causes of the improvement of the human race.' Knowledge was Condorcet's key to progress. Conversely, a decline of knowledge in society, he believed, would lead inevitably to moral and intellectual decline. He argued that tyrannies and dictatorships flourished when knowledge and literacy were withheld from the masses. He wrote of the 'genius of science and of liberty' as two interlinked aspects of a progressive society. Political freedom and knowledge, philosophical, moral and scientific, were his drivers of long-term progress. Ibid. 14, 360.

8 Ibid. 316.

9 Condorcet wrote: 'If man can predict, almost with certainty, those appearances of which he understands the laws; if, even when the laws are unknown to him, experience of the past enables him to foresee, with confident probability, future appearances.' Ibid. 316.

10 Malthus, *An essay on the principle of population* (1798) 3.

11 It is undeniable that the idea of progress has been a major concept in modernity: 'During the period 1750–1900 the idea of progress reached its zenith in the Western mind in popular as well as scholarly circles. From being *one* of the important ideas in the West, it became the dominant idea…'. Nisbet, *History of the Idea of Progress* (2009) 171.

12 Malthus, *An essay on the principle of population* (1798) 13.

13 Ibid. 13.

14 Tainter, *The Collapse of Complex Societies* (1988) 169.

15 Malthus, *An essay on the principle of population* (1798) 17.

Chapter 3 Unlocking the Future of Society

16 Jevons, *The Coal Question* (1865) xxxii. 'Since we began to develop the general use of coal, about a century ago, we have become accustomed to an almost yearly expansion of trade and employment. Within the last twenty years everything has tended to intensify our prosperity.'

17 Ibid. 186. 'The amount of power contained in coal is almost incredible…the actual useful work got from each pound of coal in a good steam-engine is that of 1,000,000 lbs falling through a foot; that is to say, there is spring enough in coal to raise a million times its own weight a foot high.'

18 Ibid. 161.

19 Ibid. 1–3.

20 Ibid. xl.

21 Ibid. xlvi.

22 Ibid.7. Jevons anticipated the fierce debates of our time about Peak Oil, Peak Coal and Peak Gas and established a significant limit to growth and progress in the finiteness of non-renewable energy sources such as the fossil fuels.

23 Ibid. 23, 25.

24 Ibid. 273.

25 Ibid. 35.

26 Britain is currently in its post-Peak Oil phase, with rapidly depleting supplies from North Sea fields. It is now a net importer of energy. This has brought about intense economic and social pressures of the kind originally conceived by Jevons.

27 'But the growth of production cannot go on *ad infinitum*; natural limits will ultimately be reached on the side both of the agricultural and the manufacturing country…'. (Ibid. 419.) Jevons reasoned that a multiplying growth and consumption rate in the country was on a collision course with a 'fixed amount of material resources'. These limits make infinite growth physically impossible.

28 Ibid. 322.

29 Hubbert, 'Nuclear Energy and the Fossil Fuels' 1956 *Drilling and Production Practice*, Publication no.95.

30 Jevons, *The Coal Question* (1865) 184–5.

31 Ibid. 187. 'there is little doubt…that a century hence the average efficiency of steam-engines will be much greater than at present…'.

32 Ibid. xlix. This could be described as the Joseph principle, alluding to the Biblical story describing how Egypt stored vast supplies of grain in a time of plenty to survive a coming time of famine and scarcity. Economic cycles, it seems, have been around for millennia.

33 Simpson, Toman, & Ayres (eds.) *Scarcity and Growth Revisited* (2005) 143.

34 Ibid. 145. What drives this virtuous circle is that prices of goods reflect their costs and these

prices determine consumption levels. Consumption levels, in turn, drive economies of scale in production. Furthermore, energy efficiency in the production process will impact on these underlying costs. Ayres defines efficiency as the 'ratio of "useful" outputs to inputs', or the ratio of actual work done to the maximum theoretical possible work output, while power is defined as 'work per unit time'. Technical progress itself he equates with increasing efficiency of converting raw resources like coal and oil into useful work. He asserts that energy-to-work conversion efficiency is fundamental to production and accounts for the main contribution of technological progress to economic growth.

35 Cardwell, *The Fontana History of Technology* (1994) 313.

36 Scott, et al, *Introduction to Technocracy* (1938) 11–12, 13–15.

37 Ibid. 'When he looks at the world [the technologist] notes that everything that moves, including the human body, does so by an expenditure of energy....Within the last hundred years we have multiplied the original output rate of that human engine by 9,000,000 in a modern conversion unit. This tremendous acceleration in the rate of doing work has altered the entire physical complex of social existence.' This technologist viewpoint sees work and production as energy conversion. Different energy converting machines create different social systems and social orders. Prior to the invention of the steam engine, the main energy converter in society was the human body, producing labour through the heat of work after gaining energy through food.

38 The Association of Peak Oil and Gas (ASPO) defines Peak Oil as 'the maximum rate of the production of oil in any area under consideration, recognizing that it is a finite resource, subject to depletion... The peak of production is normally passed when approximately half the total has been taken, termed the midpoint of depletion.' www.peakoil.net/about-peak-oil. Since the world's energy order depends on oil as its primary fuel, global peak oil threatens a serious economic reversal and is likely to initiate a period of 'creative destruction' of the existing energy order.

Chapter 4 Inventing the Future

39 Wells, *Anticipations* (1901) 5–6.

40 Ibid. 210.

41 Ibid. 6.

42 The steam engine running upon a railway, Wells stated, symbolised economic progress in the nineteenth century. Ibid. 19.

43 Ibid. 15.

44 Ibid. 36 'The determining factor in the appearance of great cities...has been the meeting of two or more transit lines, the confluence of two or more streams of trade and easy communication.'(Ibid. 41.)

45 His model of a competition between centripetal and centrifugal forces influencing the distribution of population growth is interesting. Are centripetal forces, bringing people into the cities, such as employment opportunities and access to services, from shopping and

recreation to medical facilities, etc, more powerful than centrifugal forces like the innate human love of nature and the countryside?

46 Ibid. 34.

47 Ibid. 186. 'Long before the year AD 2000, and very probably before 1950, a successful aeroplane will have soared and come home safe and sound…the new invention will most assuredly be applied to war.'

48 Ibid. 131.

49 Ibid. 35.

50 Ibid. 245.

51 Democracy 'must pass away inevitably by its own inherent conditions', (Ibid. 171.)

52 Ibid. 207.

53 Ibid. 218.

54 Ibid. 223, 230.

55 Ibid. 252.

56 Ibid. 234.

57 Ibid. 239.

58 Ibid. 258.

59 Ibid. 253.

60 Ibid. 308.

61 Ibid. 238.

62 'The trend of modern thought is entirely against private property in land or natural objects or products, and in Utopia these things will be the inalienable property of the world state.' Ibid. 63.

63 Ibid. 256, 269–71.

64 Ibid. 301.

65 Wells, *A Modern Utopia* (1905) 63.

Chapter 5 The Year the Future Arrived

66 Einstein, *Relativity* (1916) 65.

67 Ibid. 65.

68 Cox & Forshaw, *Why does E=mc²?* (2009) 5–6. 'Our grid…defines an arena within which everything exists, a kind of giant box containing all objects of the universe. We may even be tempted to call this giant arena "space".'

69 Ibid. 101.

70 Einstein, *Relativity* (1916) 39.

71 Ibid. 39.

72 Ibid. 67.

73 Hawking & Mlodinow, *The Grand Design* (2010) 99–100.

74 Bell, *Foundations of Futures Studies – Human Science for a New Era,* Vol 1 (2003) 130.

75 Crystal, D. (ed) *The Cambridge Encylopedia* (Fourth Edition) (2000) 779. 'First law: the velocity of an object does not change unless a force acts on it. Second law: a force F applied to an object of mass m causes an acceleration a according to $F = ma$. Third law: every action has an equal and opposite reaction.'

76 Ibid. 779.

77 Janiak (ed.) *Philosophical Writings* (2004) 66.

78 In *De Gravitatione*, Newton described space as 'eternal in duration and immutable in nature' (Ibid. 26.) He gives his well-known definition of absolute time and absolute space in Principia: 'Absolute, true, and mathematical time, in and of itself and of its own nature, without reference to anything external, flows uniformly and by another name is called duration….Absolute space, of its own nature without reference to anything external, always remains homogeneous and immovable.' (Ibid. 64.) Nevertheless, Newton was well aware of relative time, knowing human measurements of time were variant: 'For natural days, which are commonly considered equal for the purpose of measuring time, are actually unequal.' (Ibid. 66.) Einstein, then, did not discover relative time; rather, he abolished absolute time.

79 Hawking, *A Brief History of Time* (1988) 36.

80 Isaacson, *Einstein: His Life and Universe* (2007) 125.

81 Mermin, *It's About Time – Understanding Einstein's Relativity* (2005) 21. Reprinted by permission of Princeton University Press. 'The speed of radar is the same as the speed of light… all forms of electromagnetic radiation (light, radar, radio, x-rays, gamma rays, TV signals, for example) have the same speed in empty space.' We know that the speed of light is a constant of nature – that is the speed of light is the same for everyone.

82 Ibid. 79. The frame of reference is the point or perspective from which an object is viewed and it could be at a state of rest or inertia, or it could be a moving position.

83 What relativity theory also shows is that there is no absolute motion or fixed centre to a universe in constant motion, but only relative motion, that is, motion as observed in relation to a chosen reference frame or point. The invariant or constant in the relative universe of Einstein is the speed of light, not any given geographical location in space. Since light's speed is invariant, it is independent of all frames of reference: 'This remarkable property of light – that its speed does not depend on the frame of reference in which it is measured – is today called the principle of the constancy of the velocity of light.' (Ibid. 27.) The speed of light is thus absolute, not relative. Einstein even postulated that a train's motion is relative to the embankment it passes and, at the same time, the *embankment is in motion relative to the train* (my italics). See Einstein, *Relativity* (1916) 69.

84 Ibid. 66

85 Falk, *In Search of Time* (2008) 173.

86 Adams & Laughlin, *The Five Ages of the Universe* (1999) 116.

87 Ibid. 117.

88 Cox & Forshaw, *Why does E=mc²?* (2009) 54.

89 Mermin, *It's About Time – Understanding Einstein's Relativity* (2005) 63. Reprinted by permission of Princeton University Press. 'Any inertial observer will find that the length of a metre stick moving past him in a direction parallel to its length with uniform velocity v is less than the length of a metre stick that is stationary with respect to him…'.

90 Mermin, D. *Space and Time in Special Relativity* (1968), 55. Reprinted by permission of Princeton University Press.

91 Ibid. 123.

92 Cox & Forshaw, *Why does E=mc²?* (2009) xi. Hawking and Mlodinow place special relativity within the grand M-Theory of contemporary physics: 'there seems to be no single mathematical model or theory that can describe every aspect of the universe. Instead…there seems to be the network of theories called M-Theory.' M-Theory is a network of tested and accepted modern theories of physics which have been built on top of one another: 'The great physical theories of the twentieth century have been quantum theory (QT), special relativity (SR), general relativity (GR), and the quantum field theory (QFT). These theories are not independent of each other: general relativity was built on special relativity and quantum field theory has special relativity and quantum theory as inputs.' Hawking & Mlodinow, *The Grand Design* (2010) 58.

93 Cox and Forshaw, *Why does E=mc²?* 7.

94 *New Oxford Dictionary of English* (1998) 398.

95 Hermann Minkowski referred to the four-dimensional continuum as the 'world' and an event a 'world-point'. Einstein, 1916, p.138. In a lecture entitled 'Space and Time' delivered before the Congress of Natural Philosophers at Cologne on 21 September 1908, he stated 'No one has observed a place except at a particular time, or has observed a time except at a particular place…I call a space-point plus a time-point, i.e. a system of values, x, y, z, t, as a world-point.' This conceptualisation leads to what he described in the same lecture as 'four-dimensional physics'. (Ibid. 138.)

96 Although the fusion of space and time in relativity theory necessitated the invention of a new concept and phrase, that of space-time, it is true that the idea of time as a form of direction through space has long been implicitly assumed in the measurements of speed as a distance travelled per unit of time, for example, 120 km/hr. Our unit of length, the metre, is defined using a unit of time (the second): 'as of 1983, the metre has been defined… as the distance light travels in 1/299,792,458 of a second.' Mermin, *It's About Time – Understanding Einstein's Relativity* (2005) 21. Any object travelling through space is moving through time as well and its speed is calculated as a factor of both measurements.

97 Cox & Forshaw, *Why does E=mc²?* (2009) 64.

98 Greene, *The Fabric of the Cosmos* (2005) 49.

99 Ibid. 49.

100 The formula for calculating space-time distances is as follows: $s^2 = (ct)^2 - x^2$., where s = distance, t = time and c = speed of light. Cox & Forshaw, *Why does E=mc²?* (2009) 94.

101 Cox & Forshaw, *Why does E=mc²?* (2009) 95–96. Mermin explains the constancy of space-time distance clearly: 'Now a stationary clock moves through time at 1 nanosecond per nanosecond and does not move through space at all. But if the clock moves, there is a trade-off: the faster it moves through space – i.e. the larger v is – the slower it moves through time…It is as if the clock is always moving through a union of space and time – space-time – at the speed of light…in order to move through space as well, the clock must sacrifice some of its speed through time, in order to keep its total speed through space-time equal to 1, as required…'. Mermin *It's About Time – Understanding Einstein's Relativity* (2005) 87.

102 Adams & Laughlin, *The Five Ages of the Universe* (1999) 161.

103 Bell, *Foundations of Futures Studies – Human Science for a New Era,* Vol 1 (2003) 117.

Chapter 6 Three Arrows of Time

104 Hawking, *A Brief History of Time* (1988) 153.

105 Scientific evidence for the big bang includes not just Hubble's 1929 discovery of the expanding universe but also the 1964 discovery by Arno Penzias and Robert W. Wilson of cosmic microwave background.

106 Adams & Laughlin, *The Five Ages of the Universe* (1999) 15.

107 Ibid. 201.

108 '[P]art of time's role in the makeup of the cosmos is that it is the bookkeeper of change.' Greene, *The Fabric of the Cosmos* (2005) 225.

109 'Disorder increases with time because we measure time in the direction in which disorder increases.' Hawking, *A Brief History of Time* (1988) 156.

110 Ibid. 154.

111 Adams & Laughlin, *The Five Ages of the Universe* (1999) xix.

112 Penrose, *Cycles of Time* (2011) 53. At the level of the solar system, for example, the energy coming to earth from the sun has a lower entropy than the energy returning into space from the earth , enabling life on earth to feed off that low entropy energy before it is duly dissipated. (Ibid. 78.) Astrophysicists see a low-power death of the universe by dissipation, a possible heat death, which would be the ultimate triumph of thermodynamic principles.

113 Bell, *Foundations of Futures Studies – Human Science for a New Era,* Vol 1 (2003) 135. The universe is moving inexorably into a lower energy/higher entropy state, into greater and greater dissipation: 'Thermal equilibrium is the maximum entropy state.' Falk, *In Search of Time* (2008) 240.

114 Ibid. 141. 'The second law of thermodynamics says that if you currently have a low-entropy system, you can expect to have a high-entropy system in the future.'(Ibid. 142.)

115 Penrose, *Cycles of Time* (2011) 14–15.

116 '[E]ntropy…measures the uselessness of a certain amount of energy. There is energy in a gallon of petrol, and it's useful – we can put it to work. The process of burning that petrol to run an engine doesn't change the total amount of energy…energy is always conserved. But along the way, that energy becomes increasingly useless…And as energy transforms from useful to useless, its entropy increases all the while.' Carroll, *From Eternity to Here – the quest for the ultimate theory of time* (2011).

117 'High entropy is the natural state of being.' Greene, *The Fabric of the Cosmos* (2005) 164.

118 Adams & Laughlin, *The Five Ages of the Universe* (1999) 17.

119 'In order to survive, human beings have to consume food, which is an ordered form of energy, and convert it into heat, which is a disordered form of energy.' Hawking, *A Brief History of Time* (1988) 160.

120 'The contracting phase will be unsuitable because it has no strong thermodynamic arrow of time.' (Ibid. 161.) 'The fact that gravity is always attractive implies that the universe must be either expanding or contracting.' (Ibid. 183.)

121 Penrose, *Cycles of Time* (2011) 99.

122 Ibid. 175.

Chapter 7 On the Frontier of the Future

123 Bell, *Foundations of Futures Studies – Human Science for a New Era,* Vol 2 (2003) 317.

124 Heinberg, *Powerdown* (2004) 39.

125 Hubbert, 'Nuclear Energy and the Fossil Fuels' *Drilling and Production Practice,* Publication no.95 (1956). Zittel and Schindler suggested in 'Future World Oil Supply' that 2010 was the latest date by which Peak Oil could have occurred. www.peakoil.net/publications/International-Summer-School_Salzburg_2002.pdf. See Heinberg, *Powerdown,* 26.

126 Hubbert, 'Nuclear Energy and the Fossil Fuels' 1956 *Drilling and Production Practice,* Publication no.95. Also published online, March 8 2006 by Energy Bulletin as a 50th anniversary tribute by the Post Carbon Institue – www.energybulletin.net/node/3630.

127 Ibid. 'Consequently, the world appears to be on the threshold of an era which in terms of energy consumption will be at least an order of magnitude greater than that made possible by the fossil fuels.' Ibid.

128 Bell, *Foundations of Futures Studies – Human Science for a New Era,* Vol 1 (2003) 73. Bell later states 'The overriding purpose of futures studies is to maintain or improve human well-being and the life-sustaining capacities of the Earth, the futurist's distinctive contribution being *prospective thinking.*'(111.)

129 Ibid. 111.

130 Ibid.

131 Ibid. 167.

132 Ibid. 87.

133 Ibid. 58. This does not mean that the discipline is in disarray; on the contrary it is progressing towards growing influence and cohesion: 'Today , futures studies exists as a loosely unified set of professional activities, an emerging community of futurists, and a

growing body of shared purposes, assumptions, principles, methods, substantive knowledge, and values. It has already contributed importantly to policy deliberations and it can do so still more in the future.' (Ibid. Vol 2 329–330.)

134 '[M]any working futurists today, perhaps a majority, would agree that futures studies is an art.' Bell, *Foundations of Futures Studies – Human Science for a New Era*, Vol 1 (2003) 167.

135 Ibid. 21.

136 Ibid. 148.

Chapter 8 A Science of Time

137 Russell, *Our Knowledge of the External World* (1914), Chapter 6.

138 'Einstein's universe allows us to journey into the far future, while keeping the doors of the past firmly locked behind us.' Cox & Forshaw, *Why does E=mc²?* (2009) 4.

139 Wendell Bell describes this concept as follows: 'Modern futurists have also proposed the idea of the extended present. For example, Richard Slaughter (1993c:294), following the lead of Elise Boulding, suggests the notion of a 200-year present. Such a time span connects us directly with our parents and grandparents, our aunts and uncles and grand-aunts and grand-uncles. It also connects us with our children, grandchildren, and great grandchildren….Such a time-chain of family relationships when used to define a relevant present for social action and decision-making might help reduce the undesirable consequences of short-term thinking.' Bell, *Foundations of Futures Studies – Human Science for a New Era*, Vol 1 (2003) 140.

140 Spengler, *The Decline of the West* Vol 1: Form and Actuality (1926) 7.

141 Ibid. 8.

Chapter 9 Grounds for Foreknowledge

142 Bell, *Foundations of Futures Studies – Human Science for a New Era*, Vol 1 (2003) 68.

143 Russell, *Our Knowledge of the External World* (1914), Preface.

144 Ibid. Lecture 6.

145 Whitehead, *Adventures of Ideas* (1933) 192.

146 Peirce, *Questions Concerning Certain Faculties Claimed for Man* (1868).

147 Hawking & Mlodinow *The Grand Design* (2010) 87.

148 Cox & Forshaw, *Why does E=mc²?* (2009) 173–4.

149 Ibid. 62.

150 Bohm, *Causality and Chance in Modern Physics* (1957) 30.

151 Adams & Laughlin, *The Five Ages of the Universe* (1999) xvii–xviii.

152 Cox & Forshaw, *Why does E=mc²?* (2009) 175.

153 Bohm, *Causality and Chance in Modern Physics* (1957) 2.

154 Peirce, *Questions Concerning Certain Faculties Claimed for Man* (1868).

155 Bohm, *Causality and Chance in Modern Physics* (1957) 163.

156 Ibid. 143. Nature, declares Bohm, possesses 'an infinity of potentially or actually significant qualities…If there is no end to the qualities in nature, there can be no end to the need to probe and test all features of all of its laws…the results of scientific research to date strongly support the notion that nature is inexhaustible in the qualities and properties that it can have or develop.' (Ibid.134, 136, 140.)

157 'We cannot possibly take into account all the inexhaustibly rich properties, qualities, and relationships that exist in the process of becoming.' (Ibid. 156.) Einstein believed in universal causation. And physics certainly sees causality as both widespread in nature and inherent in its design: '[T]he causal laws satisfied by a thing, either when left to itself or when subjected to specified external conditions, are inextricably bound up with the basic properties of the thing which helps to define what it is…the causal laws that a thing satisfies constitute a fundamental and inseparable aspect of its mode of being.' Ibid. 14–15.

158 Ibid. 20.

159 'During the twentieth century, and especially within the past two decades, physics, astronomy, and cosmology have advanced rapidly and we can know understand our universe with unprecedented clarity.' Adams & Laughlin, *The Five Ages of the Universe* (1999) vii.

160 Ibid. ix–x.

161 Bohm, *Causality and Chance in Modern Physics* (1957) 1.

162 Malthus, *An Essay on the Principle of Population* (1798) 68.

163 Einstein, *The World as I See It* (1931) 29.

164 Cox & Forshaw, *Why does E=mc²?* (2009) 67.

165 Russell, *Our Knowledge of the External World* (1914), Chapter 8.

166 Ibid. Chapter 8.

167 Bohm, *Causality and Chance in Modern Physics* (1957) 5–6.

168 Ibid. 3.

169 Ibid. 6.

170 Ibid. 9.

171 Ibid. 138.

172 Ibid. 13.

173 Bell, *Foundations of Futures Studies – Human Science for a New Era,* Vol 1 (2003) 249.

174   Bohm, *Causality and Chance in Modern Physics* (1957) 17.

175   Ibid. 19.

176   Bell, *Foundations of Futures Studies – Human Science for a New Era,* Vol 1 (2003) 101.

177   'The normal terminology of "causation" takes causal influences to proceed in the past-to-future direction…'. Penrose, *Cycles of Time* (2011) 85.

178   Bohm, *Causality and Chance in Modern Physics* (1957) 3.

179   The high degree of predictability in knowledge of nature under Newtonian mechanics, derived from the predetermination of all motion of all bodies according to laws of motion, does not hold sway in a relative universe. Falk refers to the deterministic nature of Newton's laws: 'If you know the state of a system at some particular moment, you can, in principle, predict the state of the system at some arbitrary time in the future.' Falk, *In Search of Time – the history, physics and philosophy of time* (2008) 136. Yet, it has been shown that a dynamic and delicate lawfulness still inheres in the relative universe of Einstein. Einstein found plenty of evidence to believe in some form of causal determininism.

180   Crystal (ed.) *The Cambridge Encyclopedia (fourth edition)* (2000) 649.

181   Adams & Laughlin, *The Five Ages of the Universe* (1999) 15.

182   Ibid. xiii–xiv.

183   Ibid. 98.

184   'The fusion reactions that generate energy in stellar interiors must eventually come to an end as the nuclear fuel is exhausted.' (Ibid. xvi)

185   Ibid. 102. 'As a black hole leaks its mass energy away, its rate of heat loss gradually mounts, and hence the black hole cannot last forever. It is destined to evaporate into nothingness.' (Ibid. 131.)

186   'During the 39th cosmological decade, the planet evolves from a small lump of hydrogen crystal into a completely disintegrated state.'(Ibid. 106.)

187   Ibid. 33.

188   Ibid. 50.

189   Gott, *Time Travel in Einstein's Universe* (2001) 223. Samet states that the average lifespan of a species in the fossil record is 'in the range of one-million to four-million years'.Samet, *Long-Range Futures Research* (2008) 58.

190   Samet, *Long-Range Futures Research* (2008) 58.

191   Adams & Laughlin, *The Five Ages of the Universe* (1999) 99-100.

192   Clugston, *Dictionary of Science* (2004) 231.

193   Samet, *Long-Range Futures Research* (2008) 64.

194   Ibid. 203.

195   Ibid. 218.

196 Samet, 'Complexity science and theory development for the futures field' 2012 Futures (doi:10.1016/j.futures.2012.02.003).

197 Bell, *Foundations of Futures Studies – Human Science for a New Era,* Vol 1 (2003)152.

Chapter 10 An Epistemology for Futurology

198 Strong, *Strong's Exhaustive Concordance of the Bible* (1890) 44. It is thought that the Greek verb *epistamai,* to comprehend, understand or be acquainted with, is based on *ephistemi,* to stand upon, from *epi,* meaning a superimposition as in words like upon, towards and over, and *histemi,* to stand, used in applications like establish, hold up, set up, stand, etc.

199 *Concise Routledge Encylopedia of Philosophy* (2000) 246.

200 *The New Oxford Dictionary of English* (1998) 620.

201 Ibid. 1018.

202 '[E]pistemology broadly conceived may consider not just the scope of our knowledge and justified belief but also the scope of our rational belief and even of other rational attitudes toward propositions, such as certain kinds of acceptance, presumption and faith.' Audi, *Epistemology – A Contemporary Introduction to the Theory of Knowledge* (2011) 327.

203 Peirce, *The Fixation of Belief* (1877).

204 Keynes, *A Treatise on Probability* (1920), Chapter 1.

205 *Concise Routledge Encylopedia of Philosophy* (2000) 392–3.

206 'According to a long tradition, an inductive inference is an inference from a premise of the form "all observed A are B" to a conclusion of the form "all A are B".' Ibid. 392.

207 BonJour, *Epistemology: Classic Problems & Contemporary Responses* (2010), Chapter 3, The Concept of Knowledge.

208 Audi, *Epistemology – a Contemporary Introduction to the Theory of Knowledge* (2011) 176.

209 Keynes, *A Treatise on Probability* (1920), Chapter 1, "The Meaning of Probability".

210 *Concise Routledge Encylopedia of Philosophy* (2000) 430.

211 Audi, *Epistemology – a Contemporary Introduction to the Theory of Knowledge* (2011) 184.

212 Einstein, *Relativity* (1916) 139–140.

213 Ibid. 140.

214 Hawking & Mlodinow, *The Grand Design* (2010) 51. An effective theory in physics is 'a framework created to model certain observed phenomena without describing in detail all the underlying processes'.

215 Cox & Forshaw, *Why does E= mc²?* (2009) 177: 'Experiment is the final arbiter.'

216 Bohm has outlined the steps for building a plausible scientific theory. Step one: Discover regularities in nature. Step two: Make a hypothesis to explain the regularities. Step three: Make predictions about phenomena not yet contained in the initial data. Step four: Test the predictions through experiment and observation to verify the theory and prove the hypothesis to be correct. Bohm, *Causality and Chance in Modern Physics* (1957) 4–5.

217   Williams, *Problems of Knowledge – a critical introduction to epistemology* (2001) 249.

218   BonJour, *Epistemology: Classical Problems and Contemporary Responses* (2010), Chapter 3.

219   Russell, *Our Knowledge of the External World* (1914), Preface.

220   Ibid. Chapter 8.

221   BonJour, *Epistemology: Classic Problems and Contemporary Responses* (2010), Chapter 4.

222   Ibid. Chapter 4.

223   Russell, *Our Knowledge of the External World* (1914), Chapter 8.

224   Ibid. Chapter 8.

225   Ibid.

226   Ibid.

227   Ibid.

228   Ibid.

229   Ibid.

230   Hacking, *An Introduction to Probability and Inductive Logic* (2001), Chapter 4.

231   An example of a certain proposition rated 1 would be Keynes' own famous quote 'in the long run we are all dead', while an example of a probable statement, using the argument to the best explanation method, is 'it is probable that the dinosaurs were made extinct by a giant asteroid hitting the earth'.

232   Keynes, *A Treatise on Probability* (1920), Chapter 1.

233   Ibid. Chapter X1.

234   Ibid. Chapter 2.

235   Bohm, *Causality and Chance in Modern Physics* (1957) 22–24.

236   Ibid. 27.

237   Hacking, *An Introduction to Probability and Inductive Logic* (2001), Chapter 10.

238   Wilson & Keating, *Business Forecasting* (Fifth Edition) (2007) 59: 'The trend…is the long-term change in the level of the data…A seasonal pattern occurs…when there is a regular variation in the level of the data that repeats itself at the same time each year…A cyclical pattern is represented by wavelike upward and downward movements of the data around the long-term trend. Cyclical fluctuations are of longer duration and are less regular than are seasonal fluctuations.'

239   Keynes, *A Treatise on Probability* (1920), Chapter 6.

240   Ibid. Chapter 10. Hacking (2001) defined a logical probability as 'a logic relation between a hypothesis and the evidence for it'.

Chapter 11 The Key of History

241 Morris, *Why the West Rules – For Now – the Patterns of History and What They Reveal about the Future* (2011) 36.

242 Sociobiology even goes as far as to conceive of human beings as biological machines whose behaviour is predetermined.

243 Morris, *Why the West Rules – For Now – the Patterns of History and What They Reveal about the Future* (2011) 24.

244 Dostal, Cloete & Járos, *Biomatrix: A Systems Approach to Organisational and Societal Change* (2005) 3, 7.

245 Ibid. 38–9.

246 Bell, *Foundations of Futures Studies – Human Science for a New Era*, Vol 1 (2003) 135.

247 Spencer, 'Progress: Its Law and Cause, with other disquisitions' 1881 *Humboldt Library of Popular Science Literature* 1 (17): 535–536

248 Cosmologically, planets and other celestial bodies were formed from diffuse gases, Spencer argued, with increasingly concentrated and differentiated structures emerging from the initial formless condition. Gradually, cosmic entities became more integrated, their component parts mutually interacting to form a functioning whole. The same process of differentiation, he contended, happened to organisms in nature. Over time, societies, too, Spencer believed, evolved into more complex and differentiated systems with an increased economic division of labour. Even cultural products like language, he suggested, progressed from a set of simple signs to complex communication systems with their own intricate body of literature. The same held true for the evolution of the arts: 'Not only is this law thus clearly exemplified in the evolution of the social organism, but it is exemplified with equal clearness in the evolution of all products of human thought…'. (Ibid. 535–538.)

249 Ibid. 535–541.

250 Kondratieff, *The Long Waves in Economic Life* (1935) 30.

251 Ibid. 42.

252 Ibid. 34. He contended that the reason for the association of social turbulence and conflict at these points in the long waves was that they reflected economic struggle: 'Much more probable is the assumption that wars originate in the acceleration of the pace and increased tension of economic life, in the heightened economic struggle for markets and raw materials, and that social shocks happen most easily under the pressure of new economic forces…. Wars and revolutions…can be fitted into the rhythm of the long waves and do not prove to be the forces from which these movements originate, but rather to be one of their symptoms.' (Ibid. 37.) Sorokin came to similar conclusions about war and unrest: 'In the life history of nations, the magnitude of war, absolute and relative, tends to grow in the periods of expansion – political, social, cultural, and territorial – of the nation at least as frequently as in the periods of decline. In such periods of blossoming the war activities tend to reach the highest points, probably more frequently than in periods of decay…'. Sorokin, *Social and Cultural Dynamics* (1957) 565.

253 Kondratieff, *The Long Waves in Economic Life* (1935) 34.

254 Ibid.

255 Schumpeter, *Business Cycles Vol 1* (1939) 163.

256 Ibid. v.

257 Ibid. Volume 2 449.

258 Ibid. 41.

259 Ibid. 86–7.

260 Ibid. 87.

261 Ibid. 89, 91.

262 Ibid. 101.

263 Ibid. 167.

264 Ibid. 102.

265 Ibid. 148.

266 Ibid. 547.

267 Ibid. 683. Schumpeter described the money market as the headquarters of the capitalist system, with its main function being trading in credit for the purpose of financing development. (Ibid. 126.)

268 Ibid. 909.

269 Ibid. 332–3.

270 Ibid. 666.

271 Sorokin, *Social and Cultural Dynamics* (1957) 9.

272 Ibid. 10.

273 Sorokin distinguishes between two universal primary types of human culture based on their underlying logic and meaning. Ideational cultures, such as those founded in religious worldviews, mostly view reality as, in essence, non-material. By contrast, the sensory-based Sensate cultures, such as Western societies, adopt an 'agnostic attitude toward the entire world beyond the senses'.(Ibid. 27.) Other cultures are a mixture of these two basic types. But our study is focusing on the drivers of the process of social change, not different kinds of society, in order to find recurring patterns.

274 Ibid. 15.

275 Ibid. 17.

276 Ibid. 638.

277 Ibid. 640.

278 This maxim is consistent with Biomatrix theory which maintains that a system, to be sustainable and long-lasting, needs the core of a strong ethos to bind it together, that is, to be

logically integrated.

279 '[O]ther conditions being equal, during the periods when the existing culture, or the system of relationships, or both, undergo a rapid transformation, the internal disturbances in the respective societies increase; when they are strong and crystallized, the internal disturbances tend to decrease and stay at a low level....However hard living conditions may be in a given society, if the framework of its relationships and values is unshattered, no disturbances will be forthcoming....I do claim that the factor of the status of the sociocultural network of relationships and values is enough in itself to "explain" the main "ups and downs" of the curves in all the societies studied.' Sorokin, *Social and Cultural Dynamics* (1957) 602–3.

280 Ibid.17–19.

281 Sorokin defines determinism more strictly: 'By determinism in a broad sense is meant a theory that everything in the world, including man and his mind and actions, are causally conditioned, subject to the principle of the uniform and necessary relationship, and that each cause A has invariably the same effect B and is therefore invariably connected with it. More specifically, it contends that no free will exists as a factor in human behaviour.' (Ibid. 361.) As Greene has pointed out the laws of classical physics are deterministic. If the laws of physics are deterministic, and they are real, it follows determinism is real, too. 'Although you feel as if you have control over your actions, the laws of physics are really pulling the strings.' Greene, *The Fabric of the Cosmos – Space, Time and the Texture of Reality.* (2005) 456.

282 Sorokin, *Social and Cultural Dynamics* (1957) 641, 645.

283 Ibid. 642–3.

284 Samet, 'Complexity science and theory development for the futures field' 2012 *Futures* 44 (5). In the Glossary of Terms in *Long-Range Futures Research*, he contextualises teleology: 'Emergent phenomena in the civil system arise from the combined effects of both causality and teleology, which is purposeful human intervention.'

285 Sorokin, *Social and Cultural Dynamics* (1957) 57.

286 '[W]e find the same basic processes among all the societies and groups: as long as they live, there is some process of getting their living and means of subsistence; there are the processes of reproduction, birth and death; there is some kind of organization...in some form there goes on the process of learning and its transmission from generation to generation; some sort of family and marriage, magic and religion, political and economic organization, art and science, law and mores – all these and other basic institutions are found among practically all societies.' (Ibid. 656.)

287 His six main systems of truth are empiricism, rationalism, mysticism, scepticism, fideism and agnosticism.

288 Ibid. 239.

289 Ibid. 296. We see here, as in the K-waves, that time-spans can be attributed to changes in the social order. Sorokin indicates that he had noticed that considerable social disturbances are extremely common and are likely to occur in most societies on an average of every four

to seven years (603). He also noted that social disturbances tend to spread from country to country and are hardly ever confined to the country in which they originated.

290 'When the whole series for twenty-five hundred years is taken, it demonstrates the existence of long-time waves, or recurrences, of increasing differentiation and decreasing unanimity in the philosophical thought, and opposite waves of an increasing unanimity and decreasing diversity.' (Ibid. 299.)

291 Ibid. 660.

292 Ibid. 662.

293 Ibid. 282.

294 Ibid. 283. 'Instead of any linear trend, the currents rise and fall, fluctuating without any continuous tendency in the course of time.' (Ibid. 308.)

295 Ibid. 662. 'The most general pattern of the sociocultural change is that of incessantly varying recurrent processes.' (Ibid. 674)

296 Morris, *Why the West Rules – For Now – The patterns of history and what they reveal about the future* (2011) 288.

297 Ibid. 33, 35.

298 Ibid. 84.

299 Ibid. 28.

300 Schumpeter, *The Theory of Economic Development* (1934) 10.

301 Morris, *Why the West Rules – For Now – The patterns of history and what they reveal about the future* (2011) 29.

302 Ibid. 36.

Chapter 12 Seeing into the Far Future

303 Samet, *Long-Range Futures Research* (2008) i.

304 Ibid. 5. 'Civilisation is an evolutionary process in which the accumulated stock of wisdom is reflected in the institutions, culture, knowledge, information structures and socio-technological systems.'

305 Ibid. 10.

306 'Scenarios are alternative images of the future….[They] generally link qualitative narratives or storylines about the future to quantitative data in the form of tables and figures, which are often generated by computer models….Normative scenarios represent desirable future worlds…and employ feedback relationships to get from the present to the future state, which represents a goal rather than expected conditions.' (Ibid. 27, 31.)

307 Samet, *Long-Range Futures Research* (2008) 41.

308 Gott, *Time Travel in Einstein's Universe* (2001) 207–9. Gott published 'Implications of the Copernican Principle for our Future Prospects' in *Nature* in 27 May, 1993.

309 Gott, *Time Travel in Einstein's Universe* (2001) 228.

310   Samet, *Long-Range Futures Research* (2008) 41.

Chapter 13 Is Politics Predictably Unpredictable?

311   Samet, *Long-Range Futures Research* (2008) 342.

312   Ibid. 355.

313   Ibid. 413.

314   Spengler, *The Decline of the West Vol 1* (1926) xiv.

315   Ibid. Vol. 2 447.

316   Ibid. 447–8.

317   De Mesquita, *The Predictioneer's Game* (2010) xix-xx.

318   Ibid. 3.

319   Ibid. 16–17.

320   Ibid. 55, 71.

321   'In the case of people, since we cannot solve the equations that determine our behaviour, we use the effective theory that people have free will. The study of our will, and of the behaviour that arises from it, is the science of psychology. Economics is also an effective theory, based on the notion of free will plus the assumption that people evaluate their possible alternative courses of action and choose the best. That effective theory is only moderately successful in predicting behaviour because, as we all know, decisions are often not rational or are based on a defective analysis of the consequences of the choice. That is why the world is in such a mess.' Hawking & Mlodinow, *The Grand Design* (2010) 33.

322   De Mesquita, *The Predictioneer's Game* (2010) 55.

323   Sorokin *Social and Cultural Dynamics* (1957) 315.

324   Chomsky, *Government in the Future* (1970, 2005) 46–47, 64.

Chapter 14 The Search for Our Future

325   Kahn & Wiener, *The Year 2000* (1967) 2.

326   Ibid. 5.

327   Ibid. 7

328   Ibid. 5.

329   Ibid. 6.

330   Ibid.

331   'With a set of alternative futures and scenarios that lead to them by alternative routes, one may see better what is to be avoided or facilitated, and one may also gain a useful perspective on the kinds of decisions that may be necessary, and the points in time after which various branching-points will have been passed.' Ibid.

332   Ibid. 6–7. '[M]odern history in particular does seem to have certain cyclical or ebb-and-

flow characteristics in time periods as short as decades.' (Ibid. 12.)

333 Ibid. 122.

334 Ibid. 220.

335 Ibid. 122.

336 Meadows, Randers & Meadows, *Limits to Growth: the 30-Year Update* (2004) ix.

337 Ibid. x.

338 Ibid.

339 '[T]he land area...required to provide the resources (grain, feed, wood, fish and urban land) and absorb the emissions (carbon dioxide) of global society.' Meadows, Randers & Meadows, *Limits to Growth: the 30-Year Update* (2004) xiv.

340 Ibid. xi.

341 Ibid. xii.

342 Ibid. xiv.

343 Ibid. xviii.

344 Ibid.

345 Ibid. xix.

Chapter 15 Future of the Future

346 Samet, 'Complexity science and theory development for the futures field' 2012 Futures (doi:10.1016/j.futures.2012.02.003).

347 Penrose, *Cycles of Time* (2011) x, Preface.

348 'By 1997, futures studies had most of the characteristics of a separate field of enquiry. It had full-time professionals, networks of communication and formal professional associations, university futures courses and a few entire educational programs, conferences and meetings, hundreds of publications annually, shared purposes, a set of identifiable futurist methods, underlying assumptions, and shared exemplars that stand within a growing body of knowledge. Moreover, it had a thirty-plus-year recent history of development, a sense of a futurist community, and important individual and organizational pioneers who were increasingly recognized for their contributions.' Bell, *Foundations of Futures Studies – Human Science for a New Era, Vol 1*(2003) 71. Bell speaks of the methodological diversity in the futures field. From scenarios to Delphi surveys, from trends analysis to global simulation models, from futures workshops to global futures activism, there is a treasury of futuristic methods and approaches. Bell describes the scenario as the pre-eminent method of futures research. Bell, *Foundations of Futures Studies – Human Science for a New Era, Vol 2* (2003) 319.

349 Hawking & Mlodinow, *The Grand Design* (2010) 5.

Chapter 16 Invasion of the Future

350 'The Hubble constant is a measure of the rate of expansion of the Universe. It is found by dividing the rate v at which galaxies recede from our own by their distance r….It is estimated to be between 50 and 100 kilometres per second per megaparsec.' Clugston, *Dictionary of Science (2nd Edition)* (2004) 312. See also NASA's description of the Hubble Constant at http://map.gsfc.nasa.gov/universe/uni_expansion.html

351 Greene, *The Fabric of the Cosmos* (2004) 229.

352 Janiak (ed.), *Newton: Philosophical Writings* (2004) 135.

353 Interestingly, the word 'evolve' contains only the letters of the word 'love'.

354 Russell, *Our Knowledge of the External World* (1914), Chapter 8.

355 'If we don't act when we have the chance, that chance may not come again…one of the things we should understand about time is that we have just a little.' Gott, *Time Travel in Einstein's Universe* (2001) 235; 239.

Appendix 1 The Ten Greatest Predictions of all Time

356 Churchill, *The Gathering Storm* (1948) 77.

Appendix 2 Evidence Supporting the Theory of Relativity

357 Einstein, *Relativity* (1916) 144.

358 Einstein & Minkowski, *The Principle of Relativity*, (1920) 162.

359 Cox & Forshaw, *Why does E=mc²?* (2009) 4; 235.

360 Hawking, *A Brief History of Time* (1998) 35.

361 Hawking & Mlodinow, *The Grand Design* (2010) 99.

362 Cox & Forshaw, *Why does E=mc²?* (2009) 52.

363 Adams & Laughlin, *The Five Ages of the Universe* (1999) 130.

364 Falk, *In Search of Time – the History, Physics and Philosophy of Time* (2008) 167.

365 Cox & Forshaw, *Why does E=mc²?* (2009) 184

366 Ibid. 219

Appendix 3 Why the Uncertainty Principle is Overrated and Misconstrued

367 Hawking, *A Brief History of Time* (1988) 59–60.

368 Ibid. 60, 63–5.

369 Ibid. 13.

370 Bohm, *Causality and Chance in Modern Physics* (1957) 145.

371 Ibid. 147–8.

372 'Each level enters into the substructure of the higher levels, while, *vice versa*, its characteristics depend on general conditions in a background determined in part in other levels, both higher and lower, and in part in the same level.' Ibid. 140.

373 Ibid. 51.

374 Kaku, *Physics of the Future* (2011) 177.

375 Bohm, *Causality and Chance in Modern Physics* (1957) 50.

376 Ibid. 51.

377 Ibid. 84, 87, 95, 100.

378 Ibid. 50.

379 Hawking, *A Brief History of Time*, (1988) 65.

380 Hawking & Mlodinow, *The Grand Design* (2010) 103.

381 Ibid. 72–73.

382 Ibid. 131.

383 Ibid. 67–8.

REFERENCES

Adams, F & Laughlin, G. 1999. *The Five Ages of the Universe.* New York: Simon and Schuster.

Audi, R. 2011. *Epistemology – A Contemporary Introduction to the Theory of Knowledge (Third Edition).* New York: Routledge.

Bell, W. 2003. *Foundations of Futures Studies – Human Science for a New Era,* Vol 1 and Vol 2. New Brunswick: Transaction Publishers.

Bohm, D. 1957. *Causality and Chance in Modern Physics.* London: Routledge & Kegan Paul Ltd.

BonJour, Laurence. 2010. *Epistemology: Classic Problems and Contemporary Responses.* (2nd Edition). New York: Rowman & Littlefield Publishers, Inc.

Cardwell, D, 1994. *The Fontana History of Technology.* London: Fontana Press.

Carroll, S. 2011. *From Eternity to Here – the quest for the ultimate theory of time.* Oxford: Oneworld Publications.

Chomsky, N. 1970 (2005). *Government in the Future.* New York: Seven Stories Press.

Churchill, W. 1948. *The Gathering Storm.* London: The Reprint Society.

Clugston, M. 2004. *Dictionary of Science (2nd Edition).* London: Penguin Books.

Concise Routledge Encyclopedia of Philosophy. 2000. London: Routledge.

Cox, B. & Forshaw, J. 2009. *Why does E=mc²?* Cambridge, MA: Da Capo Press.

ed. Crystal, D. 2000. *The Cambridge Encylopedia* (Fourth Edition). Cambridge: Cambridge University Press.

De Caritat, J.A.N (Marquis de Condorcet). 1795. *Outlines of an historical view of the progress of the human mind.* Moscow: Book Renaissance.

De Mesquita, B.B. 2010. *The Predictioneer's Game.* New York: Random House.

Dostal, E., Cloete, A. & Járos, G. 2005. *Biomatrix: A Systems Approach to Organisational and Societal Change*. Third Edition. Cape Town: Mega Digital.

Einstein, A. 1916. *Relativity*. St Petersburg, Florida: Red and Black Publishers.

Einstein, A. 1931. *The World as I See It*. New York: The Wisdom Library.

Einstein, A and Minkowski, H. 1920. *The Principle of Relativity*. Reprint by University of Toronto Libraries Collection.

Falk, D. 2008. *In Search of Time – the History, Physics and Philosophy of Time*. New York: Thomas Dunne Books.

Gott, J.R. 2001. *Time Travel in Einstein's Universe*. New York: Houghton Mifflin Company.

Graf, P. & Grondin, S., et al. 2006. *Timing the Future – the case for a time-based prospective memory*. New Jersey: World Scientific Publishing Co.Pty. Ltd.

Greene, B. 2004. *The Fabric of the Cosmos – Space, Time and the Texture of Reality*. New York: Vintage Books.

Hacking, I. 2001. *An Introduction to Probability and Inductive Logic*. Cambridge: Cambridge University Press.

Hawking, S. 1988. *A Brief History of Time*. London: Bantam Books.

Hawking, S. & Mlodinow, L. 2010. *The Grand Design*. London: Bantam Press.

Heinberg, R. 2004. *Powerdown*. Gabriola Island: New Society Publishers.

Hubbert, M.K. 1956. Nuclear Energy and the Fossil Fuels. *Drilling and Production Practice 95* – Shell Development Company. (Published online as 50th anniversary tribute in the Energy Bulletin, March 2006, Post Carbon Institute http://www.energybulletin.net/node/13630)

Isaacson, W. 2007. *Einstein: His Life and Universe*. London: Simon & Schuster.

ed. Janiak, A. 2004. *Newton: Philosophical Writings*. Cambridge: Cambridge University Press.

Jevons, W.S.1865. *The Coal Question*. Reprints of Economic Classics. New York: Augustus M. Kelley.

Kahn, H & Wiener, A.J. 1967. *The Year 2000*. New York: The

Macmillan Company.

Kaku, M. 2011. *Physics of the Future*. New York: Doubleday.

Keynes, J.M. 1920. *A Treatise on Probability*. London: MacMillan & Co.

Kondratieff, N. 1935. *The Long Waves in Economic Life*. Whitefish, MT: Kessinger Publishing's Legacy Reprints.

Malthus, T.R. 1798. *An essay on the principle of population*. Oxford: Oxford University Press. 3.

McCraw, J.K. 2007. *Prophet of Innovation: Joseph Schumpeter and Creative Destruction*. London: Belknap Press of Harvard University Press.

Meadows, D., Randers. J & Meadows, D. 2004. *Limits to Growth: the 30-Year Update*. White River Junction, Vermont: Chelsea Green Publishing Company.

Mermin, N.D. 1968. *Space and Time in Special Relativity*. Illinois: Waveland Press, Inc.

Mermin, N.D. 2005. *It's About Time - Understanding Einstein's Relativity*. Princeton: Princeton University Press.

Morris, I. 2011. *Why the West Rules – For Now – The Patterns of History and What They Reveal about the Future*. London: Profile Books.

Nisbet, R. 2009. *History of the Idea of Progress*. New Brunswick: Transaction Publishers.

Peirce, C.S. 1868. *Questions Concerning Certain Faculties Claimed for Man*. London: Mobile Lyceaum (2011).

Peirce, C.S. 1877. *The Fixation of Belief*. London: Mobile Lyceaum (2011).

Penrose, R. 2011. *Cycles of Time*. New York: Alfred A. Knopf.

Russell, B. 1914. *Our Knowledge of the External World*. London: Routledge Classics. (Published in the Taylor & Francis e-library 2009.)

Samet, R. 2008. *Long-Range Futures Research*. North Charleston: BookSurge Publishing.

Samet, R. 2012. Complexity science and theory development for the futures field. *Futures* 44 (5).

Schumpeter, J. 1934. *The Theory of Economic Development*. New Brunswick: Transaction Publishers.

Schumpeter, J. 1939. *Business Cycles – A Theoretical, Historical and Statistical Analysis of the Capitalist Process.* Chevy Chase, MD: Bartleby's Books.

Scott, Howard, et al. 1938. *Introduction to Technocracy.* New York: Technocracy Inc

Simpson, R.D., Toman, M.A. & Ayres, R.U. ed. 2005. Resources, Scarcity, Technology and Growth. *Scarcity and Growth Revisited.* Washington: Resources for the Future.

Slaughter, R. ed. 2005. *The Knowledge Base of Futures Studies: Professional Edition.* Indooroopilly (Australia): Foresight International (CD-ROM).

Sorokin, P. 1957. *Social and Cultural Dynamics.* Boston: Porter Sargent Publisher.

Spencer, H. 1881. Progress: Its Law and Cause, with other disquisitions. *Humboldt Library of Popular Science Literature* 1 (17): 535-562.

Spengler, O. 1926. *The Decline of the West.* New York: Alfred. A. Knopf.

New Oxford Dictionary of English, 1998. Oxford: Oxford University Press.

Strong, James. 1890. Strong's Exhaustive Concordance of the Bible. Nashville: Abingdon Press.

Suddendorf, T., Addis, D.R., & Corballis, M.C. 2009. *Mental time travel and the shaping of the human mind.* Philosophical Transactions of the Royal Society. London: Royal Society Publishing.

Tainter, J.A. 1988. *The Collapse of Complex Societies.* Cambridge: Cambridge University Press.

The New Oxford Dictionary of English. 1998. Oxford: Oxford University Press.

Wells, H.G. 1901. *Anticipations.* London: The Floating Press (a 2008 reprint from the 1902 edition) (www.thefloatingpress.com)

Wells, H.G. 1905. *A Modern Utopia.* EbooksLib (http://www. ebookslib.com).

Whitehead, A.N. 1925. *Science and the Modern World.* New York: The Free Press.

Whitehead, A.N. 1927–8. *Process and Reality (Corrected Edition).*

New York: The Free Press.

Whitehead, A.N. 1933. *Adventures of Ideas.* New York: The Free Press.

Williams, M. 2001. *Problems of Knowledge – a critical introduction to epistemology.* Oxford: Oxford University Press.

Wilson, J.H. & Keating, B. 2007. *Business Forecasting* (5th Edition). New York: McGraw-Hill.

INDEX